Alaska's Inside Passage

Ann Chandonnet
Photography by Don Pitcher

COMPASS AMERICAN GUIDES
An imprint of Fodor's Travel Publications

Compass American Guides: Alaska's Inside Passage

Editor: Jennifer Paull
Designer: Moon Sun Kim
Compass Editorial Director: Paul Eisenberg
Compass Creative Director: Fabrizio La Rocca
Editorial Production: Bethany Cassin Beckerlegge
Photo Editor and Archival Researcher: Melanie Marin
Map Design: Mark Stroud, Moon Street Cartography
Cover Photo: Don Pitcher

First Edition
ISBN 1–4000–1480–8
ISBN–13: 978–1–4000–1480–4

The details in this book are based on information supplied to us at press time, but changes
occur all the time, and the publisher cannot accept responsibility for facts that become outdated
or for inadvertent errors or omissions.

This book is available at special discounts for bulk purchases for sales promotions or premiums.
Special editions, including personalized covers, excerpts of existing books, and corporate
imprints, can be created in large quantities for special needs. For more information, write to
Special Markets/Premium Sales. 1745 Broadway, MD 6-2, New York, New York 10019, or
e-mail specialmarkets@randomhouse.com.

Compass American Guides, 1745 Broadway, New York, NY 10019
PRINTED IN CHINA
10 9 8 7 6 5 4 3 2 1

To the memory of my dear 'Gram,' who always wanted to see Alaska.

C O N T E N T S

Sidebars and Topical Essays

Literary Extracts

Maps

Get ready for a sensory immersion in a splendid landscape.

INTRODUCTION

The mesmerizing effects of light on water, quickly changing skies, rocky promontories, thundering cataracts, silvery mists, dense foliage. Get set for a sensory immersion in nature's splendor.

If the painters of the 19th-century Hudson River school could have cruised along Alaska's Inside Passage they would have thought they'd died and gone to artists' heaven. Enraptured as they were with the American wilderness, imagine how they would have reacted to the Alaskan landscape, which makes the Catskill Mountains look like Central Park. The Hudson River school painters believed art capable of moral and spiritual transformation. Alaskans believe nature has those abilities.

Europeans discovered Alaska when a Russian expedition sighted the territory in 1741. The name "Alaska" comes from the Aleut word *alyeska*, meaning "Great Land." The Russians began their incursions in the Aleutians and Commander Islands. Wherever the *promyshlenniki* (fur hunters-traders) could not easily obtain sea-otter pelts themselves, they forced the Aleuts to hunt for them. Gradually they explored eastward. Within 20 years the *promyshlenniki* reached Kodiak Island, enslaving Native Alaskans as they went. When Aleksandr Baranov became the chief manager of the Russian-American Company, he expanded operations south, establishing a permanent post at Sitka in 1804. The Native Tlingits, uneasy about their occupiers, often fought back. Only a continent-wide smallpox epidemic in the late 1830s finally quashed their resistance.

After years of negotiations, the United States purchased what was known as "Russian-America" in 1867. The Russians were willing to sell because they faced increased competition from British and American whalers and traders, because expansion was difficult, and because they had decimated the sea-otter population. Secretary of State William H. Seward believed that Alaska would more than pay for itself in furs, walrus ivory, fish, jade, gold, and timber. Alaska was purchased for $7.2 million—or two cents an acre. The vast territory was classed as a department and put under the control of the U.S. Army. For the next 15 years the military ruled by misrule. Despite the natural riches of the place, no one paid much attention

The Coast Mountains form the backdrop for Haines's Portage Cove.

except prospectors, missionaries, educators, and visiting scientists. Ernest Gruening, Alaska's governor in the 1940s and '50s, called it an "era of total neglect."

In 1911, forty-four years and eight presidents after the Alaska Purchase, President Theodore Roosevelt inquired into the needs of its indigenous inhabitants. He asked Navy lieutenant George Thornton Emmons to write a report. Emmons first described the Eskimos, Athabaskans, and Aleuts of the Arctic and Interior. Then he turned to the people of southeast Alaska and wrote:

> "The Tlingit, Haidas, and Tsimsheans, who occupy the narrow continental shore and adjacent islands, number some 6,000 souls and live in comparative comfort under very favorable conditions in large, well-built villages along the coast and channel ways. Here the climate is mild and healthful, wood and water are on every hand, fish life is abundant, and game is more than sufficient for their wants. They are intelligent, honest, and good workers; an accumulative, thrifty people, quick to learn, and anxious to improve their condition." All they asked, wrote a sympathetic Emmons, who had lived among them, is to have what American citizens have: "educational advantages . . . , protection in their rights to hold property and to locate mineral lands, citizenship when qualified, and the establishment of hospitals at central points."

The Organic Act of 1884 had provided for a territorial governor and law enforcement—although not for representation in Washington, D.C. The territory was neglected, despite lobbying efforts by Judge James Wickersham and others. Alaska's first congressional delegate was finally appointed in 1906. Teddy Roosevelt, convinced by Emmons's arguments, convened a territorial legislature in 1912. At that time the total population, Native and Caucasian, numbered about 70,000. Few improvements were made in taming the wilderness until the threat of World War II brought in military personnel, and bases were established at Anchorage, Whittier, Fairbanks, Nome, Sitka, Delta Junction, and Kodiak, and Dutch Harbor islands in the Aleutians. Alaskans continued to struggle to gain the right to govern themselves until January 3, 1959, when "The Last Frontier" finally became the 49th state.

(following pages) The Point Retreat lighthouse toughs it out on Admiralty Island, near Juneau.

In the meantime, the southernmost part of Alaska—the 500-mile-long, curved, lush coastal strip called the Panhandle—had become its best-known region. This area had milder winters than the Arctic and was easily accessible from major ports like San Francisco, Seattle, Port Townsend, and Vancouver. Steamships began to carry tourists to the Panhandle's scenic waterways in the 1880s. The Klondike Gold Rush of 1896–98 further piqued the curiosity of those wishing to see the frontier. The Inside Passage was one of the main routes to the Klondike gold fields, and after stampeders had blazed the trail, more and more tourists ventured north on summer steamship jaunts. They used the new portable Kodak camera to record their scenic adventures.

In the Inside Passage's winding waterway, 1,500 islands act as bulwarks against large surges from the open Pacific. When a storm rages in the exposed Gulf of Alaska, for example, creating 11-foot seas, the seas in sheltered Stephens Passage may measure a calmer 4 feet.

ALASKA'S INSIDE PASSAGE

The phrase "Inside Passage" came into use in 1885, when Lieutenant Commander Richardson Clover USN used it to indicate the saltwater passage connecting Tongass Narrow and Clarence Strait. However, it quickly came to mean all the passages between Sitkian Island and Disenchantment Bay. And sometimes the phrase is used to embrace the passages immediately north of Vancouver.

Alaska has no "tales of the city." The closest we come is when a visitor asks for a map of the state, looks it over, and quickly hands it back, shaking his head, asking, "Where are the roads?" True, paved highways are few and far between here, but don't let that stop you. Living along the Inside Passage, I've come to appreciate the Norse phrase for the sea, "the whale road." Once you've seen killer whales flashing across the surface or humpbacks giving a saucy wave of their flukes, the phrase takes on a fresh, dramatic meaning.

Walk across the wetlands of Gustavus in May and relish the pleasure of striding knee-deep through chocolate lilies, violet-blue lupine, and hot pink shooting stars. Snowshoe across Mendenhall Lake in January until you reach the

With this Treasury Warrant, the U.S. snapped up Alaska for two cents an acre.

glimmering blue spires of the glacier's mile-wide front. Dive into a remote lake and see if the loons will swim up to inspect you. Rest on velvety moss. Listen to woodpeckers and Swainson's thrushes. Look for swan nests or moose as you soar in a six-seater Piper Cherokee.

In more than 30 years in Alaska, I've found that some of the best times are to be had on foot, in a kayak, standing at the rail of a ferry or excursion vessel, or exploring back roads. After all these years I still find it difficult to describe this place. All I can say is, "Come. See for yourself." You won't be sorry.

■ How to Use this Book

To aid in planning your visit to Alaska's Inside Passage, these pages put a number of tools at your disposal.

The chapters are arranged in order of a fantasy cruise from south to north with a fishhook loop near the end: Ketchikan, Wrangell, Petersburg, Juneau, Skagway, Haines, Glacier Bay, and Sitka.

A site map shows the locations of historic buildings, museums, totems, monuments, and other points of interest in each city or town.

Each chapter kicks off with frequently asked questions (FAQs).

Kid Stuff sections suggest activities that appeal to children—some participatory, some as observers. (Note: Children should always be accompanied by an adult.)

Each town chapter includes a walking tour of moderate length. These walks are laid out in an easily followed, point-to-point manner.

Each town chapter also includes Brief Excursions and Longer Outings sections. Listings in Brief Excursions cover local sights and activities that can be enjoyed in an hour to three hours—anything from a short hike or tour of a museum to a Tlingit canoe-carving workshop. Longer Outings point you to side trips that take anywhere from four hours to several days.

Finally, the comprehensive index includes activities, historical figures, and attractions. Venues that are accessible to travelers with limited mobility are indexed under "accessible."

To Excursion Inlet

Old Sitka State
Historic Site

Sitka National
Historical Park

Sitka

To
Juneau

Killisnoo
Neltushkin

Sumdum
Windham

Goddard

ADMIRALTY

ISLAND

BIROKA I

Baranof

Tyree

1

NECKER
ISLANDS

BARANOF

ISLAND

Chatham
Strait

Stephens Passage

Inside Passage

Kake

Frederick

Sound

Fanshaw

UNITED STATES
CANADA

COAST

Glacier

River

Port
Armstrong

Port Herbert

Port Alexander

TONGASS

KUIU

ISLAND

KUPREANOF

ISLAND

Kupreanof

Petersburg
Scow Bay

Mt Burkett
9,730 ft

Devils Thumb
9,077 ft

Kates Needle
10,023 ft

BRITISH
COLUMBIA

Cape Ommaney

Ferry

Kelu
Strait

2

Cape Decision

CORONATION
ISLAND

Port
Protection

NATIONAL

Summer
Strait

MITKOF
ISLAND

ALASKA

Castle Mtn
7,330 ft

Stikine

Cape Pole

KOSCIUSKO
ISLAND

ZAREMBO
ISLAND

Wrangell

Stikine

WARREN
ISLAND

Edna Bay

Tokeen

Coffman
Cove

WRANGELL
ISLAND

Mt Whipple
5,745 ft

M
O
U
N
T
A
I
N
S

HECETA
ISLAND

ETOLIN
ISLAND

Anan Creek
Wildlife
Observatory

NOYES
ISLAND

FOREST

Klawock

Thorne Bay

Santa Anna

Bell Island

3

BAKER
ISLAND

LULU
I

SAN
FERNANDO
ISLAND

Craig

Hollis

Meyers Chuck

Mt John Jay
7,499 ft

Cape
Bartolome

Bucareli Bay

Waterfall

Kasaan

Cape Lookout

SUEMEZ
ISLAND

Sulzer

Helm Bay
Loring

Totem Bight
State Historical Park

FORRESTER
ISLAND

Hydaburg

Ketchikan

Misty

Fiords

Hyder

Stewart

SUKKWAN
ISLAND

Ward Cove
Saxman

National

Alice Arm

DALL

ISLAND

LONG I

Cordova Bay

PRINCE OF WALES ISLAND

Clarence Strait

REVILLAGIGEDO

ISLAND

Behm Canal

Monument

Kalgani

Metlakatla
Annette

4

Cape Muzon

GRAVINA
ISLAND

ANNETTE
ISLAND

UNITED STATES
CANADA

Dixon
Entrance

Cape Chacon

DUKE
ISLAND

Revillagigedo Channel

Cape
Fox

Cape Knox

Cape Northumberland

ZAYAS I

PEARSE I

Arrandale

DUNDAS
ISLAND

Port
Simpson

Ferry

QUEEN
CHARLOTTE
ISLAND

Halda

Rose Point

Inside Passage

Georgetown
Mills

5

Masset

STEPHENS I

**Prince
Rupert**

Port Clements

Ferry

To
Skidgate, BC

PORCHER
ISLAND

Hunts
Inlet

Elevation
in feet

10,023
9,000
7,000
5,000
4,000
3,000
2,000
1,000
Sea Level

**LOWER
SOUTHEAST**

Miles
0   25   50

Kilometers
0   25   50   75

NATIVES IN FULL POTLATCH
DANCING CUSTOME
COPYRIGHT 1906 BY
CASE & DRAPER
56

THE LAND
AND THE PEOPLE

The steep wooded hills, icy glaciers, drenched forests, and narrow shoreline of southeast Alaska have so shaped the cultures here that it is difficult to consider habitat and residents separately.

"Land is the simplest form of architecture," Frank Lloyd Wright wrote. Everywhere along the Inside Passage, veils of shifting mist glide up steep ravines of dark spruce like animated chalk drawings. Martens swim between rocks at high tide, snacking on mussels. In dozens of small harbors, boats tug at their lines like horses ready for a gallop. Mating bald eagles join talons and free-fall, spinning wildly, each daring the other to let go. But neither is "chicken," and the pair plummets into an alder "hell" so tangled that they must walk awkwardly to the nearest clearing before they can take to the sky again.

Southeast Alaska is chiefly a land of mild, even temperatures and heavy rainfall. The water falls from evergreen needle to leaf to sphagnum, and then seeps through thin acid soils. Murmuring spruce and hemlocks, cedars, and yews flourish in dense stands from water's edge to tree line. Some trees soar more than a hundred feet into the clear air, while the forest floor beneath them is a tangle of alder, blueberry, prickly rose, thorny devil's club, ferns, mosses, Deer Heart, skunk cabbage as tall as a man, uncountable creeks, and periodic roadblocks of giant trunks twisted and felled by the wind, their exposed root systems the height of a garage. Sitka black-tailed deer, shrews, bears, red-breasted sapsuckers, and flying squirrels inhabit these forests.

■ A RARE RAIN FOREST

Alaska's rain forest is the northern portion of a continuous forest pressed against the warm vapors of the ocean currents and guarded from the interior's freezing temperatures by the Pacific Coast Ranges. Old-growth temperate rain forest like this is the rarest forest type on earth—much rarer than tropical rain forest.

A Tlingit man and woman pose in traditional dancing costumes, ca. 1906.

GLACIER FACTS

- Alaska has more active glaciers than the rest of the inhabited world combined. Four percent of Alaska is under ice.

- Glaciers form from snow falling and accumulating over a period of years. When snowflakes fall, they are 80 percent air. As the snow layers accumulate, the flakes compress into rounded grains. Additional weight from the deepening snow eventually presses these grains into blue ice with less than 20 percent air content. It can take hundreds of years to compress snow into glacial ice.

- Glaciers advance on a layer of meltwater than can be as thin as a sheet of paper.

- Ice crystals within glaciers can grow as large as a football.

- Iceworms really do exist. You might spot some of these black crawlers if you're walking on a glacier, but they're so threadlike that they may not wow you.

This unique habitat, capable of producing swamps on steep slopes, stretches from Yakutat to Seattle. Some biogeographers contend that the rain forest extends far beyond the Inside Passage—all the way from Kodiak Island to Monterey, California. The western hemlock and Sitka spruce forest reaches from Oregon to Prince William Sound. National borders divide this mighty arc, but it remains an ecological whole. Both British Columbia and downtown Juneau experience an average annual rainfall of 100 inches.

Temperate rain forest means jaw-dropping scenery at every point of the compass, at every bend in the trail. It means lush, undeveloped real estate and 50 shades of green.

■ THE GLACIERS

At the height of the Wisconsin glaciation, about 20,000 years ago, things were a bit different. Most of southeast Alaska was covered by an undulating plain of ice so thick that only mountain peaks higher than 5,000 feet pierced through. As the glaciers advanced and retreated, their grinding and polishing slowly carved out U-shaped valleys. Where they opened to the sea they created magnificent fjords rivaled only by those of Norway—the fjords that would later beckon to explorers.

About 12,000 years ago the climate began to change, and V-shaped valleys were dug out by streams, rivers, and landslides. After another 4,000 years the land began to rise, lifting areas like the Mendenhall Flats above sea level. (Glacial rebound at Mendenhall is about 0.60 inches per year.) Tectonic forces have also raised parts of the Inside Passage, although it is less subject to seismic temblors than Kodiak or San Francisco.

As glaciers recede, living things colonize the exposed raw rock in a particular succession. First, mosquitoes deposit their larvae in melt puddles. Next, breezes carry spores of mosses or the parachute-equipped seeds of fireweed. Other seeds are dropped by birds. These grow and pave the way for more plant life. After about a decade, new homesteaders arrive: horsetails, mountain avens, and lichens. Creatures on the scene range from hover flies to Dolly Varden char, sticklebacks, nervous shrews, and blustering wolverines. The glacier's blue tongue melts away, leaving a spoor of damp rubble. After another 25 years thriving alder and willow thickets take root in this rubble. These pioneer shrubs fix nitrogen and create soil, in turn allowing a mixed spruce and black cottonwood forest to flourish a mere century after the tongue of ice withdrew.

Although British Columbia and Cape Cod have not felt the weight of large glaciers for 10,000 years, southeast Alaska shook hands with the Little Ice Age about 2,000 years ago. In places like Glacier Bay, advancing glaciers reached their maximum forward thrust as recently as the mid-1700s. Since then most Inside Passage glaciers have receded. For more information on glaciers, *see* the Glacier Bay National Park chapter.

■ NATIVE ALASKANS

With the land so difficult to cross, early peoples used glaciers as frozen portages, and stuck to routes where rivers and streams gave access to the backcountry. The ocean waterways, except along the outer coast, are protected from the sea's breakers, so Pacific Northwest peoples could easily row their canoes on the gentle swells.

The wet weather might make the place seem uninhabitable until you consider its wealth of fish, berries, furs, marine mammals, shellfish, waterfowl, copper, wood, and fresh water. With this bounty close at hand, man could easily preserve foodstuffs for the winter, allowing ample leisure for storytelling, celebration, and art. It was this combination of resources and leisure that attracted and held the coastal Indians living north of Washington State: the Salish, Nootka, Kwakiutl,

Bella Coola, Haida, Tsimshian, and Tlingit. These peoples survived in isolation for centuries, developing distinctive institutions and patterns of behavior. (The Salish, Nootka, Kwakiutl, and Bella Coola reside in Canadian territory and, although related to the Haida, Tsimshian, and Tlingit, will not be discussed here.)

Each people harvested a broad territory. The Haida (pronounced *high-dah*) lived on the Queen Charlotte Islands and the southern part of Prince of Wales Island. They were renowned for the size and excellence of their cedar canoes. The Tsimshian (*sim-shee-ahn*) claimed fishing villages on the lower Skeena River and hooligan fishing grounds on the lower Nass. They took advantage of seasonal foods by efficiently drying and smoking fish and meat, rendering oil from fish and seals, and preserving berries and wild crab apples in oil. The Tlingit (*kling-git*) occupied the largest territory, the coast from Yakutat Bay to Cape Fox. Like the Tsimshian, the Tlingit lived in plank houses during the winter. They built smoke-houses and lean-tos covered with bark or mats at hunting and fishing sites.

How large were these populations? That's difficult to say. A survey of the Tlingit made in 1839 for the Hudson's Bay Company, taken after a smallpox epidemic had

Haida dancers in potlatch regalia.

raged for three years, and not including Sitka or the settlements from the Alsek River to Controller Bay, counted a population of 5,455 "Kolosh" (as the Russians called them). In 1967 the Bureau of Indian Affairs counted 320 Haida living in the villages of Craig and Hydaburg and 8,482 Tlingit. The BIA estimated that "considerable numbers" of Alaskan Natives were living in Anchorage, Seattle, and Oakland, California, "where chance for employment is greater."

■ NATIVE TRADITIONS

Each Native people, the Haida, Tsimshian, and Tlingit, was divided into groups of clans called *moieties*. The Tsimshian have four moieties (which they call *phratries*): Wolf, Eagle, Raven/Frog, and Killerwhale/Bear/Fireweed. The Tlingit have two moieties, the Raven/Crow and the Eagle/Wolf—depending upon the time period. The Haida also have two, the Eagle and Raven. All three peoples are matrilineal, meaning that legitimacy and moiety descend from the mother, and young boys are trained by their uncles (their mother's brothers) rather than their fathers.

From time immemorial, a river's mouth was the prize site for a Native village because of the wealth of salmon, herring, and hooligan that congregate there annually, and the seals, whales, and birds that follow the fish. (Fish at river mouths are always in top shape; fish farther up the waterway cease eating in their spawning quest, and are less desirable.) Plank houses were laid out following the curve of the shoreline, usually with the chief's house in the center. Each house had a name like Moon House, Beaver House, or House Where People Always Want to Go. If the owner was rich enough to commission a frontal totem, this pole was erected between the house and the shore, facing approaching canoes.

Chiefs bore both traditional and personal names. Traditional names included Sigai ("the open sea") or Nankilstlas ("he whose voice is obeyed"). A traditional name was handed down with the office. The chief of the Wrangell area bore the traditional name of Shakes (Se.ks).

Northwest Coast peoples lived in relative isolation, although there were occasional intertribal raids. Peace was the norm, however, and neighbors kept in touch with each other through trade in goods transported in their impressive seagoing canoes. Iridescent abalone came from as far away as Monterey Bay. Other goods—some from inland populations—included elk hides, moose skins, copper, mountain-goat wool, and ornamental shells. Trade was so important that trading partners often married into each other's family.

A HARMONIOUS PATTERN

. . .The coast-line of Alaska is about twenty-six thousand miles long, more than twice as long as all the rest of the United States. The islands of the Alexander Archipelago, with the straits, channels, canals, sounds, passages, and fiords, form an intricate web of land and water embroidery sixty or seventy miles wide, fringing the lofty icy chain of coast mountains from Puget Sound to Cook Inlet, and, with infinite variety, the general pattern is harmonious throughout its whole extent of nearly a thousand miles. Here you glide into a narrow channel hemmed in by mountain walls, forested down to the water's edge, where there is no distant view, and your attention is concentrated on the objects close about you—the crowded spires of the spruces and hemlocks rising higher and higher on the steep green slopes; stripes of paler green where winter avalanches have cleared away the trees, allowing grasses and willows to spring up; zigzags of cascades appearing and disappearing among the bushes and trees; short, steep glens with brawling streams hidden beneath alder and dogwood, seen only where they emerge on the brown algae of the shore; and retreating hollows, with lingering snow-banks marking the fountains of ancient glaciers. The steamer is often so near the shore that you may distinctly see the cones clustered on the tops of the trees, and the ferns and bushes at their feet.

—John Muir, describing the Inside Passage on his first trip to Alaska in 1879,
Travels in Alaska, 1915

Trade was central to amassing wealth. With wealth, a chief could prove his social status by holding a feast called a potlatch. The potlatch, or "giving," is a formal distribution of goods that reasserts claims to property and privilege. At these events, which could go on for five days or more, chiefs distributed everything from coppers (shield-shaped copper objects) to furs to carved oil dishes. Anthropologist H. G. Barnett wrote in 1938, "Virtue rests in publicly disposing of wealth, not in its mere acquisition and accumulation."

Most missionaries and some early anthropologists did not see any virtue in huge giveaways. They saw them as economic suicide, "pagan" or "megalomaniacal."

As new trade goods came into the country with the arrival of Europeans and Americans, potlatch gifts began to include button blankets, Hudson's Bay blankets, samovars, treadle sewing machines, gramophones, sacks of flour, and pool tables. Elaborate oratory was employed to welcome invited guests, narrate tribal history, and pay compliments to the chief. Family heirlooms bearing clan crests would be paraded, and songs, dancing, and feasting were all part of the festivities. Every potlatch required such an abundance of food that leftovers would be carried away. Typical potlatch dishes were smoked salmon, dried fish, berries mixed with hooligan oil, and oil and wild crab apples mixed with snow.

The cultures of all three groups included potlatches—events expected of clans or high-ranking figures. Potlatch occasions included weddings, naming a child, or erecting a totem pole. Haida parents might hold a potlatch to establish the position of a young boy as heir presumptive. The Tlingit potlatch was often a series of rituals to mourn the death of a chief. The first served to reward the opposite moiety for conducting the funeral rites. The second introduced the new chief. The third celebrated the building of the new chief's house. The fourth might raise a mortuary pole in memory of the deceased chief.

How long has all this been going on? Pacific Northwest peoples have lived along this coast for 7,000 to 10,000 years. One site at Blue Jacket Creek on Masset Inlet has yielded evidence 3,500 years old of woodworking tools such as wedges, hammers, adzes, and chisel blades.

Fringed ceremonial blankets such as this are worn by Tlingits to significant events such as funerals.

The Tsimshian are distinguished from the Haida and Tlingit in two important ways. First, their language seems to have no relationship to any other language, in either North America or Asia. Second, the Tsimshian did not settle in Southeast Alaska until historic times. This people originally lived along the Nass and Skeena rivers in British Columbia. In the 1830s some relocated to the Hudson's Bay Company trading post at Port Simpson. In 1857 a young Anglican missionary, William Duncan, came to educate the Tsimshian. In 1862, to separate his flock from liquor and other unhealthy influences, Duncan led a party of 50 back to their original lands and established a model village called Metlakatla. In 1881 Duncan had a falling out with his church leaders. The U.S. government gave him permission to relocate his community on Annette Island, 18 miles from Ketchikan. Duncan and 825 Tsimshian relocated in 1887 and built New Metlakatla. The island is the only Indian reservation in Alaska.

■ THE EXPLORERS' IMPACT

In 1774 the Spaniard Juan Perez became the first European to trade with the Haida. In the forty years following 1787, the previously isolated Haida were visited

by hundreds of European and American ships. Explorers included Captain James Cook, Captain George Vancouver, Lieutenant (later Commander) Nathaniel Portlock, George Dixon, John Meares, Captain Joseph Billings, Commander Edward Belcher, Hudson's Bay Co. executive Sir George Simpson, Alexander Baranof, navigator Andrei Khlebnikov, Nikolai Rezanov (one of the founders of the Russian-American Company), naval officer Iurii Fedorovich Lisiansky, French sea captain Etienne Marchand, naval officer/fur trader Camille de Roquefeuil, and Captain Robert Gray. Between 1787 and 1809 at least 64 American ships traded off the Northwest Coast.

The start of something big: an early example of canned salmon.

These explorers brought blue cloth, blue beads, and iron to trade—but they also brought new diseases. In the late 1830s the first of a series of smallpox epidemics ravaged the Northwest Coast, carrying off about half the Haida by the close of the decade. In the mid-1850s Haida men began looking for work in Victoria and Nanaimo. Many villages were abandoned by 1900.

In prehistoric times villages were sometimes relocated following fires or to elude enemies bent on capturing slaves. But as European and American newcomers arrived, they sometimes appropriated the sites of villages and forced villagers to move away. Some relocated in the constant jockeying among chiefs for the best position relative to a trading post. Later reasons for moving included opportunities for schooling children, attending

This 1897 board game played off popular perceptions of the Klondike Gold Rush.

church, or working for cash. Traditional fish-camp sites were abandoned as tribal members instead labored at canneries during the summer.

■ NEW CLAIMS TO SOUTHEAST ALASKA

In the late 18th century, Russian interests attempted to move down the coast through Prince William Sound and into the Inside Passage, but they met with fierce Tlingit resistance and a challenge from the British. The chief manager of the Russian-American Company, Alexander Baranof, was anxious to establish a trading foothold in Southeast Alaska before another nation beat him to it. In 1794, Baranof dispatched a fleet of 500 one- to three-man *bidarkas* (Native

ALASKA EXCURSIONS   STEAMSHIP "SPOKANE"

SEASON 1903

LUNCH

SOUP—CLAM BROTH

VEAL CUTLETS BREADED, TOMATO SAUCE

STEWED LAMB, PARISIENNE POTATOES

BAKED CHEESE ON TOAST   APPLE FRITTERS

COLD ROAST BEEF   ROAST CHICKEN   ROAST PORK

CORNED TONGUE   HAM

COSMOPOLITAN SALAD

RICE   CAULIFLOWER   BAKED, BOILED AND MASHED NEW POTATOES

GREEN APPLE PIE   MINCE PIE

CURRANT BUNS   ASSORTED PASTRY

STEWED APRICOTS   STEWED PEARS   STEWED PRUNES

PRESERVED PEACHES   ASSSORTED JAMS

ORANGE ICE   FRUITS IN SEASON

CHEESE—SWISS   EDAM   OREGON CREAM   ROQUEFORT   AMERICAN

TOASTED CRACKERS

TEA   COFFEE   CHOCOLATE   COCOA   MILK

WEDNESDAY, JULY 8TH

The early cruises were stylish too; this menu dates from 1903.

kayaks) to Icy Bay and Yakutat Bay. The party's hunt was successful, bringing back 900 sea-otter skins. But they encountered the English ships *Discovery* and *Chatham,* and Captain George Vancouver contested their claim to the area.

Natalia Shelikov, head of the Northwestern American Company, grew concerned about the British protests. She wrote to the Russian empress, "Now is the time to settle the question as to the boundary line between the Russian possessions and the English as there is a danger that they might make us abandon them altogether." Settlements in Cook Inlet and Prince William Sound were at risk, as well as the potential south of Lituya Bay, a promising territory she described as "the places of our dreams and imagination."

Baranof was instructed to explore farther south and bury tablets claiming the territory. During the summer of 1795 he visited Chilkat and Sitka. Delayed by injuries, storms, and shipwrecks, Baranof was not ready to set up a permanent outpost at Sitka until four years later.

The Tlingit cleverly played the British against the Russians. In 1799 Baranof watched as traders from Britain and the United States bartered for 2,000 sea-otter furs. The Russians had little in the way of trade goods, while the Tlingit managed to trade for woolen cloth, handfuls of beads, and excellent muskets and pistols manufactured in Boston and London.

But Baranof believed he had laid a "strong foundation" for Russia's occupying southeast Alaska, and sailed back to Kodiak in April 1800. Two years later, on the morning of June 26, 1802, Tlingit warriors overwhelmed the Sitka fort, burning it and killing many Russians, Native hunters, and their families. The Russians, under Baranof, fought back by retaking the fort in 1804. The Tlingit nation did not immediately give up. They destroyed the Russian settlement at Yakutat in August 1805, and attempted to destroy the fort at Konstantinovsk in Prince William Sound. But gradually the Sitka Tlingit made peace with the Russians, re-establishing trade by exchanging halibut for fishhooks.

KETCHIKAN

Often the first port of call on cruises of Alaska's Inside Passage, Ketchikan acts as a scenic introduction to the coastal rain forest and the hardy folk who call it home. Even before you reach town, the sight of deer or bears swimming across Wrangell Narrows will let you know you're not in Kansas any more. You'll know, as photographer Ansel Adams put it, that you are "closer to elemental things."

Like Juneau, Ketchikan is sandwiched between a hard place, Deer Mountain, and a wet channel, Tongass Narrows. Gravina Island lies just offshore. This geographical situation means that the Ketchikan airport is on Gravina, connected to town by a ferry—although a bridge may be in the works. The town itself meanders like a silk scarf for six miles along the available strip of coast, with wooden stairways standing in for streets when the slopes get especially steep.

Ketchikan perches on the southwest side of a larger island, Revillagigedo—often shortened to Revilla. Like Haines, Skagway, Juneau, Wrangell, and most other towns of the Inside Passage, Ketchikan is surrounded by Tongass National Forest. As if that weren't bounty enough, Ketchikan is only about 30 miles west of the 2.2 million-acre wilderness of Misty Fiords National Monument.

How to access this nearby acreage? Take a leaf from the locals who board floatplanes and charter vessels as casually as residents of the Big Apple hail a cab or swing aboard the subway. Floatplanes or charter boats can whisk you to destinations such as Misty Fiords or Prince of Wales Island (20 miles west of town), known for its caves.

Ketchikan uneasily wears the title "rain capital of Alaska," bestowed in recognition of its average annual precipitation: 160 inches. The 15,000 friendly residents take fog and damp in stride, wearing knee-high rubber boots everywhere, even to the theater, and staging slug races during the Blueberry Arts Festival. They practically purr as they take deep breaths of some of North America's freshest air—washed clean by frequent downpours of "liquid sunshine."

■ KETCHIKAN THEN

Humans have found this area habitable for at least 10,000 years. In July 1996 paleontologists investigating On Your Knees Cave on northern Prince of Wales Island

Genteel-looking Creek Street was once the red-light district's main drag.

KETCHIKAN

0   500   1,000 Feet

------- Trail or Stairs

To
Alaska State Ferry,
Totem Bight State Park, 10 mi.
Settler's Cove, 16 mi.
Ward Lake Recreation Area, 7 mi.

Walker-Broderick House

Schoenbar Rd

Grant St

Schoenbar Trail

Ketchikan Creek

Park Ave

Eagle
Center

City
Park

Fair St

Bridge

Hospital

Bawden St

Cedar St

Pine St

Grant St

Edmond St

Harris St

Venetia Way

Married Man's
Trail

Totem Heritage Center/
Public Restrooms

Front St Stair

Tongass Ave

Main St

Library &
Tongass Historical
Society Museum

Cape Fox Lodge/Tram

Tram

Woodland Ave

Deermount St

Eagle Totem

Thundering Wings
Eagle Park

Front St

Dock St

Post
Office

Whale
Park

Bawden St

Creek Street Boardwalk

Dolly's House

To
Deer Mountain
Hatchery
& Restrooms

Cruise Ship
Terminals

Mission St

Main St

Stedman St

Deermount St

Ketchikan Visitor
Information Center

Front St

Spruce Way

Mill St

Southeast Alaska
Discovery Center

Goldbelt Alaska Cruises

To
Saxman Village and
Totem Park, Beaver Clan House
& Libby Cannery

Cruise Ship
Terminals

Thomas
Basin

Thomas St

N
W   E
S

Tongass Narrows

GRAVINA
ISLAND

FAQs:

What does the town's name mean?

There's some debate on this point, but it's likely derived from a traditional Tlingit term, *Kitchik-him,* which has etymological associations with eagles and rivers. However, a 1924 volume tracing the early explorer George Vancouver's journeys says the name means "wedged," a reference to Gravina Island, which appears wedged against the larger Revilla Island. Local historians assert that *Kitschk* means "the thundering wings of an eagle." Further, they believe that *Kitschkhin* translates as "Kitschk's stream," after a Tlingit man from Cape Fox or Tongass who established a seasonal fishing camp near Ketchikan Creek in prehistoric times.

Slices of Ketchikan life.

Do people live here year-round?

Yes. Or, as Dave Kiffer, director of Historic Ketchikan Inc., puts it: "There are wetter places on earth, but hardly anyone chooses to live there."

Where is the Tongass?

Everywhere—that is, any spot that is neither private property nor Native corporation land. The Tongass National Forest encompasses most of the land in the Inside Passage, 17 million acres.

What do you call baby salmon?

When they hatch from fertilized eggs, they are "fry." When they begin feeding, call them "fingerlings"—but don't call them late to dinner. When they reach four to eight inches, they become "smolts."

Ketchikan's waterfront in the early 20th century.

discovered the partial skeleton of a man whose remains were dated at more than 10,000 years old. Finds like this are rewriting archaeological theories about the peopling of America.

As elsewhere in the Inside Passage, place names around Ketchikan hold history like brimming cups. Intriguing names often reflect the adventures of European and Russian explorers in the 18th and 19th centuries. "Saxman," for example, refers to Samuel Saxman, an American teacher lost with two other men during the winter of 1886 while seeking a new village site. The name of Ketchikan's island, Revillagigedo, reveals that Spanish explorers were among those searching for new territory along this rugged coast. Spain sent three separate expeditions (1774, 1775, and 1779, the third led by Juan Francisco de la Bodega y Quadra). Bodega y Quadra named Revillagigedo for the Count of Revilla Gigedo, viceroy of Mexico in the late 1700s.

The British captain George Vancouver ventured into Stikine River territory in August 1793. On the afternoon of August 21, a party of Stikine Tlingit approached his vessels from the western shore of Clarence Strait. An inferior chief, Kanaut, was allowed to board Vancouver's ship and offered to introduce the cap-

THE HAIDA WORLD

To the Haida the world was like the edge of a knife cutting between the depths of the sea, which to them symbolized the underworld, and the forested mountainside, which marked the transition to the upper world. . . . On the one side they faced treacherous ocean currents; on the other, dense forests.

Perhaps because of their precarious position, they embellished the narrow human zone of their villages with a profusion of boldly carved monuments and brightly painted emblems signifying their identity. Throughout their villages these representations of the creatures of the upper and lower worlds presented a balanced statement of the forces of their universe. Animals and birds represented the upper world of the forest and the heavens, while sea mammals, especially killer whales, and fishes symbolized the underworld. The transition between realms was bridged by such amphibians as frogs, beavers, and otters. Hybrid mythological creatures, such as sea grizzlies and sea wolves, symbolized a merging of cosmic zones.

—George F. MacDonald, *Chiefs of the Sea and Sky*, 1989

tain to the region's most powerful chief, Ononnistoy. On August 31 Ononnistoy himself arrived, and was treated to a display of fireworks and served bread, molasses, rum, and wine.

Spanish explorers failed to establish a permanent settlement in Stikine territory. That task was accomplished by an Irishman, Mike Martin of Portland, Oregon, who wanted to capitalize on the area's fisheries. A saltery had been erected at the mouth of Fish Creek in 1883, and the first salmon cannery opened in 1886. Martin came to the area in 1885 and acquired 160 acres from Chief Kyan. In 1888 Martin obtained 640 acres of land from a Haida named Paper Nose Charlie, built a cannery, and filed incorporation papers in 1900. (Another version of the story says that Charlie was a Kwakiutl Indian, and that he wore a paper nose after a Wrangell Tlingit bit off his nose in a violent altercation.)

The Inside Passage experienced several gold rushes in the early 1900s, and the new town became a supply center for miners. Salmon canning also took off. In 1924 Ketchikan canned 125,000 cases of salmon, and in the 1930s there were more than a dozen canneries in operation. So much salmon was harvested here that Ketchikan was crowned "salmon capital of the world" and briefly became Alaska's largest city. But overfishing took its toll, hastened by mismanagement by

the Fish and Wildlife Service of the Department of the Interior. The salmon canning industry began to wane in the 1940s.

During World War II, logging and pulping stepped up as the main sources of income. Western hemlock was harvested for shipping containers, furniture, railroad ties, and mining timbers. Yellow cedar, with its even grain, was harvested for flooring, doors, sashes, and cabinets. By 1949 Ketchikan had a large sawmill and a box factory. In 1953 the Ward Cove pulp mill opened northwest of town, processing spruce and hemlock for the production of rayon and cellophane. For decades the mill was the biggest employer in southeast Alaska.

■ KETCHIKAN NOW
map page 32

Today debates simmer between those who wish to clear-cut timber and those who want to preserve old-growth forest. The future of logging in the area is uncertain, and may depend—as in decades past—on who is in power in Washington. Meanwhile, Ketchikan's main industries are fishing and tourism. The latter began to flourish when flights

Local traffic: seaplanes and cruise ships in the Tongass Narrows.

were instituted between Seattle and Ketchikan by Pan American Airways in 1940. Ketchikan is now just 90 minutes by jet from Seattle, making it accessible to the Lower 48 in less time, and at a lower cost, than any other part of Alaska.

Mariculture is also gaining a foothold in the local economy. When Ketchikan Pulp's mill closed in 1997, community leaders promoted a floating upwelling system to encourage shellfish farming. Known as FLUPSY, this nursery system helps reduce oyster spat mortality and can halve the time needed to cultivate an oyster crop for market. There are now 10 shellfish farming sites near Ketchikan.

Ketchikan describes itself as "three miles long and three blocks wide," an indication of how it follows the waterfront from the ferry terminal to Thomas Basin and beyond. In summer Ketchikan bustles much like Juneau and other Inside Passage towns: floatplanes taking off and touching down, fishing boats offloading at canneries as gulls scream for scraps, ferries and cruise ships noisily arriving. No matter the weather, residents carry on, picnicking, dipnet fishing, and playing baseball in the rain.

■ WALKING TOUR

Begin at the "Welcome to Alaska's First City" sign near the cruise-ship docks. A walking-tour map is available at the nearby **Ketchikan Visitors Bureau** (131 Front Street; 907-225-6166; www.visit-ketchikan.com). Stroll along Mission Street to Whale Park to see the Chief Kyan Totem. At the far end of the park is the Kadjuk or Chief Johnson Totem, a replica of a 1901 original; it represents the heritage of the Kadjuk House of the Raven clan. (Kadjuk is a mythical bird based on the golden eagle.) Turn left for the Raven Stealing the Sun Totem, which stands just outside the **Tongass Historical Museum** (629 Dock Street; 907-225-5600), which shares a building with the town library. The museum preserves an important collection of original totems retrieved from abandoned Tlingit village sites. Its displays, which range from stone tools to contemporary art, give insights into the Tlingit, Tsimshian, and Haida cultures.

Turn back toward Whale Park to reach the bridge across Ketchikan Creek. (Look for a sculpture standing in the water paying tribute to salmon.) Cross the bridge to **Creek Street**. This wooden thoroughfare, built on pilings around 1900, was the main drag of a flourishing red-light district until the early 1950s. The district was reached by the so-called Married Man's Trail from Park Avenue. During Prohibition some of the bawdy houses became speakeasies, with liquor from

KID STUFF

- Watch a Native artist carve a totem, canoe, or paddle in the Edmund C. DeWitt Carving Center at Saxman Village (907-225-4846).

- Get an eyeful of top timber athletes at the Great Alaskan Lumberjack Show (Spruce Mill Way; 907-225-9050). They demonstrate speed climbing, axe throwing, and carving with chain saws, plus the almost comedic balancing act of log rolling. There are three performances daily; each lasts an hour and 15 minutes. The grandstand has handicapped access and is heated and covered.

- Look for spawning salmon from the Creek Street boardwalk. Kings spawn from the end of July through August; coho spawn from Thanksgiving through Christmas.

Outside rowed in on high tides. Many of Creek Street's 20 houses have been restored to suit more genteel businesses like the marvelously cluttered **Parnassus Books** (5 Creek Street; 907-225-7690). Get a hint of Prohibition-era mischief at **Dolly's House Museum** (24 Creek Street; 907-225-6329). This former brothel displays the possessions of the madam Big Dolly Arthur. If the sheriff came calling, she could dispose of bootleg whiskey through a trapdoor into the creek.

If you're a view hound, turn back toward the bridge to board the funicular ($2) to the **West Coast Cape Fox Lodge** (800 Venetia Way; 800-544-0970). From the hill you can look out over the town and the Tongass Narrows. The hotel's lobby and staircase are decorated with beautifully carved wooden panels in the Tlingit form-line tradition. Exit on Venetia Avenue to see the circle of modern totems, "The Council of the Clans."

Continue along Venetia to Park Avenue. Turn right on Park, and follow it to City Park and the **Deer Mountain Tribal Hatchery and Eagle Center** (1158 Salmon Road; 800-225-5158). Here you can see king and coho fingerlings, rainbow trout and steelhead, and photograph eagles up close. There is a narrated tour. Cross over a pedestrian bridge to **Totem Heritage Cultural Center** (601 Deermount Street; 907-225-5900). More than 30 unrestored totem poles stand here, some nearly two centuries old, plus fragments of others retrieved from deserted Tlingit and Haida villages. The center also hosts classes in beading, basketry, carving, and silver engraving.

This walking tour, mostly on level ground, requires three to four hours. If you're here on a weekend in July, you could check out the *Fish Pirate's Daughter* by the First City Players, a long-running melodrama based on Ketchikan's history (1716 Totem Way; 907-225-4792).

■ BRIEF EXCURSIONS

Walk to the corner of Main and Pine streets to view the **Chief Kyan Totem**. Legend has it that anyone touching this pole will receive money within 24 hours—so now's the time to buy that lottery ticket. There are some noteworthy early-20th-century buildings near this intersection too. Check out the turreted Monrean House (500 Main Street), a 1904 Queen Anne–style residence. Two blocks away at 541 Pine Street stands the Craftsman-style Walker-Broderick House (c. 1916). Both are listed on the National Register of Historic Places.

Rent a kayak and launch at Bar Point Basin marina. Paddle into Thomas Basin and then up Ketchikan Creek at high water. The trip takes two to three hours. **Southeast Exposure** (515 Water Street, 800-827-1607) rents kayaks and offers guided trips; beginners will get instruction.

Two of Ketchikan's striking totems: Chief Kyan (left, ca. 1900) and Chief Johnson (right).

Head into the woods with an **Adventure Kart Expedition** (Cape Fox Tours, 907-225-4846; www. capefoxtours.com). First, you'll board a jet boat to reach a private site. Next, spend two hours splashing through mud puddles on an 8-horsepower dune buggy especially made for back-country use. Drivers must be licensed, but youngsters may ride as passengers. You might spot deer, ravens, and eagles on this trip. Then you'll be driven back to town by bus.

How about **a guided fly-fishing tour** to White River to fish for steelhead and silver and pink salmon? Cape Fox Tours runs a trip that takes care of the 45-minute van ride each way, with three hours of fishing; waders and gear are provided. More than half the guides are Tlingit or Haida, and happy to chat about their traditional way of life (907-225-4846; www.capefoxtours.com).

Ketchikan also bills itself as "one of the top 100 small arts communities in the United States." Don't miss its **art galleries** and arty events such as August's Blueberry Arts Festival. Of particular interest is the Saxman Village Store (2711 Killerwhale Avenue, 907-225-4421), which sells locally made totems, masks, carvings, and button blankets (ceremonial blankets decorated with buttons). Two blocks away is the Saxman Arts Co-op (907-225-1640), with similar offerings. The Winter Arts Faire, held annually the weekend after Thanksgiving, is a great opportunity to purchase local arts and crafts.

Take the **Explore Historic Ketchikan Tour** (Cape Fox Tours, 907-225-4846; www.capefoxtours.com) to George Inlet. This narrated bus trip takes you to the Libby, McNeill, and Libby Cannery (1913–58). In addition to learning about the

MISTY FIORDS

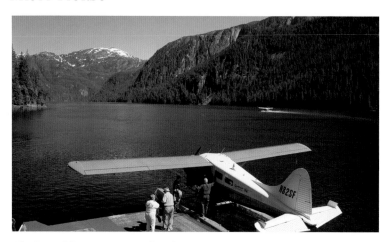

Play "Misty" for me: Hopping a floatplane in Misty Fiords.

Nearly as large as Glacier Bay National Park and Preserve but not as well known, Misty Fiords National Monument offers a whopping 2.2 million acres of breathtaking wilderness playing hide-and-seek in the billows of shifting mist. Some of the protected land covers the east coast of Revillagigedo Island, while the rest lies on the mainland between the Behm and Portland canals. Shaped by glaciers and annually drenched by 150 inches of snow and rain, this land was set aside as protected territory in 1978. Steep cliffs rise as much as 3,000 feet above the ocean.

Although the Inside Passage is less seismic than the Aleutian Chain, it occasionally experiences earthquakes and once had active volcanoes. If you're interested in seeing evidence of Alaska's steamy history, consider a 3½-hour charter catamaran trip that includes New Eddystone Rock, a giant chunk of basalt known as a volcanic core. The rock juts straight out of the water in the middle of Behm Canal.

Like Glacier Bay National Park, Misty Fiords is so large that you may prefer to view it from the air. Or you could rent a Forest Service cabin; some have ocean moorings while others, set on alpine lakes, are equipped with their own small boats. Whatever your taste, the monument is superb from any angle. The Ketchikan–Misty Fiords Ranger District is the best source of up-to-date information on boating and camping in "Misty" (907-225-2148; www.fs.fed.us/r10/tongass). Private tour operators offer flightseeing, hunting trips, and photographic excursions.

cannery's history, you'll see demonstrations of logging, gold mining, and commercial fishing—a rare combination for an Inside Passage tour. Pull up crab pots while learning which creepy-crawlies are keepers. There is a brief photo stop at Saxman Native Village on the return trip.

■ LONGER OUTINGS

Feast your eyes on dozens of totems. If the totems in the Tongass Historical Museum and the Totem Heritage Cultural Center described above have only sparked your appetite, there are dozens more in a pair of parks outside town. Start at the **Southeast Alaska Visitor Center** (50 Main Street; 907-228-6214). Displays include contemporary totem poles and a realistic, life-size fish camp diorama. Then drive or hike south 2.5 miles on the Tongass Highway to **Saxman Village Totem Park** (907-225-4846). The two dozen totems at this site were brought in the 1930s from abandoned villages on Tongass, Cat, Pennock, and Village islands and from Kirk Point. The most photographed pole is topped with a figure of Abraham Lincoln; it may refer to the U.S. revenue cutter *Lincoln*. Finally, drive nine miles north on the Tongass Highway to the 13-acre **Totem Bight State Historical Park** (907-247-8574). Flickers, the only woodpeckers to dine on the ground, may dart about as you take the short woodland trail through hemlocks to this lovely spot. The replica community house gives a real sense of dim, cedar-scented Tlingit interiors. Some of the park's 15 Haida and Tlingit totems are topped with the watchman figure, a lookout typically wearing a woven spruce-root hat. If you don't have a car, you can get to Saxman Village by city bus or taxi. (However, if you want to enter its Beaver Clan House, you must be on a Cape Fox Tour.) City buses do not go to Totem Bight.

Soak up incredible scenery in **Misty Fiords National Monument**. You can reach the park via a 30-mile floatplane or boat ride from Ketchikan. (Allow several hours for a flightseeing trip and at least a full day for a boat tour.) You'll have a good shot at spotting wildlife, as Misty Fiords is a haven for brown and black bears, Sitka deer, mink, river otters, and the occasional moose. The waters of Behm Canal teem with humpbacks, orcas, porpoises, sea lions, and seals. If you'd like to kayak, you can rent a kayak from Southeast Exposure (800-827-1607) for an independant adventure or sign up with Southeast Sea Kayaks (800-287-1607) for a five-hour guided trip. Twenty-foot tides make beach camping unsafe, but Forest

EARLY INSIDE PASSAGE CRUISES

Sightseers came to the Inside Passage hard on the heels of the map-makers and missionaries who spread word of its magnificent vistas. By the 1880s visitors were regularly taking the Pacific Coast Steamship Company's vessels north from San Francisco or Portland. By 1886 these trips were so popular that the steamship company doubled its summer sailings.

Many of the earliest passengers penned enthusiastic, detailed books or articles that defrosted the notion of "Seward's ice box" and drummed up tourism. Eliza Scidmore, correspondent for the St. Louis *Globe Democrat* and the *New York Times*, compiled her *Journeys to Alaska* after an 1883 paddlewheeler cruise. She reported on the trade in shining bracelets pounded from silver dollars, spoons steamed from mountain goat horn, and intricate baskets.

By the end of the 1800s Native artists were responding to the tourist influx by producing items that could be transported easily, such as totem poles less than a yard high, baskets in the shape of tea kettles, and tiny silver spoons. Since tourists didn't appreciate Native art, traditional works were often demeaned as grotesque curios. A 1912 Alaska Steamship Company brochure promised tourists "crude gropings toward art by a primitive people."

Souvenirs were an attraction, but so were glaciers. The panorama began at Wrangell, with the Stickeen Glacier on the nearby eponymous river. Then, as ships steamed toward Skagway they passed a dazzling parade of icy giants: Patterson, Bairds, Young, Yosemite, Toyatt, Windom, Taku, Eagle, Auk, Meade, and Dewey. Glacier Bay was ringed with the Muir, Pacific, Hugh Miller, and Geikie glaciers. These were set off by smaller glaciers and dramatic waterfalls too numerous to name.

World War I put a crimp in cruising, but the industry quickly revived. The Inside Passage route was endlessly praised. A 1930 brochure of the Pacific Steamship Company gushed, "For over one thousand miles the World's Smoothest Waterway unwinds its silver screen of scenic wonderland, each immense foot of celluloid disclosing a gem of ocean and mountain beauty more thrilling than the one just rolled into the background of our memory." (A 9- to 12-day cruise of 2,350 miles cost $100, with meals.)

Cruise-ship traffic continues to grow. In 1992, 263,047 visitors arrived in Ketchikan by cruise ship; by 2003 the number had risen to 757,374. In 2004 Juneau received more than 800,000 cruise-ship visitors; if 5 ships dock, that means 13,000 arrivals in a single day. Projections for 2007 put the number of cruise passengers in Juneau at a million.

Scooting out of town in sea kayaks.

Service cabins can be reserved. Goldbelt Alaska Cruises (800-228-1905; www.mistyfjord.net) is one of the best-known local boat and flightseeing operators. See the "Misty Fiords" sidebar for more information.

Board a plane or ferry for the 12-mile journey to **Metlakatla on Annette Island,** home of the Tsimshian tribe and the state's only Native reservation. The island was once a Canadian settlement led by missionary William Duncan, but in 1891 Congress turned it over to the Tsimshian. Now the town feels like a quiet pioneer village. Activities include a tour of the community and the Duncan Cottage Museum (1891), a dance performance, and artist demonstrations (907-886-8687). Excursions take 4 to 12 hours.

Try spelunking in one of the deepest caves in the United States. About 850 square miles of limestone lie beneath the Tongass National Forest. As water seeps into the limestone, it erodes sink holes, fissures, and cave systems to form a "karst landscape." Board the ferry to Hollis on Prince of Wales Island, then drive three hours to access the **El Capitan Underground Cave Tour**. El Capitan is the largest surveyed cave in Alaska, with 12,000 feet of mapped passageways. You'll see limestone and marble formations, but the real treasure here is bones from bears, river otters, and other mammals, some dating back 12,000 years. Access to the cave is considered difficult, and there's lots of uneven footing. If you're up for the challenge, you'll need to reserve a Forest Service guide two days in advance (907-828-3304). Free tours are offered Thursday through Saturday in summer; no children under age seven are allowed. Hard hats are provided. If you don't have a car, you can contact TLC Cab (907-826-2966) for the drive from Hollis.

W R A N G E L L

Like Sitka, Wrangell has witnessed several eras in its past—eras of Russian exploration, British fur trading, Russian occupation, economic boom accompanying gold rushes, and American logging and fishing. Like Juneau's, much of its downtown stands on rock fill. As in Treadwell, destructive fires in 1906 and 1952 robbed it of its historic core.

Wrangell is a quiet, friendly place, compact enough to tour on foot in a few hours. The inner harbor curves its protective arms around Chief Shakes Island. In summer the air thrums with the perfume and engine sounds of shrimp- and salmon-processing. Wrangell's history is closely tied to that of the Stikine River seven miles north. The Stikine is North America's fastest navigable river; it was a prehistoric Tlingit trade route, then a supply corridor for the 19th-century Stikine and Cassiar gold rushes. In 1897–98 it became famous as one of the routes to interior Canada during the Klondike gold rush. Wooded hillsides backed by snow-capped mountains form a striking backdrop—old hat to residents, but thrilling for arriving visitors as their ships draw close to the dock jutting out into Zimovia Strait.

■ WRANGELL THEN

The threads of Wrangell intertwine with the web of Tlingit prehistory. Legend has it that bands of hunters spreading across the Arctic and Subarctic regions of Alaska grew in size until they needed new territory. As they explored farther south, they migrated down great rivers to the coast. Perhaps 8,000 years ago, when much of the southeast was covered by sheets of ice, one adventurous group in British Columbia attempted to descend the swift, 330-mile Stikine River. Soon their way was blocked by a great glacier—too rough to cross and too wide to portage around. The cold, swirling river disappeared into a big hole. But where did the hole lead?

An elder volunteered to paddle his canoe into the frightening opening. "I will send a smoke signal if I come out safely," the man promised. He daringly aimed his craft at the gaping maw of the ice cave and was instantly out of sight. The people waited anxiously. Then the signal came. He was safe! The rest of the band

The Eagle Totem guards the Tribal House of the Bear.

Petroglyph Beach
Wrangell Beach

Zimovia Strait

Airport Rd
Airport and Terminal
Airstrip

Evergreen Ave

Mt Dewey 400ft
Mt Dewey Trail
Library/Internet Access

Muskeg Meadows Shoting Range, 1 mi.

Spur Rd

St Rose Catholic Church
2nd Ave
St Michael St

Alaska Ferry Terminal
Third St
1st Ave
Reid St
Second St
McKinnon St
Grief St
Church St
Mission St
St Michael St

Post Office
Visitor Center
Public Restrooms
James and Elsie Nolan Center/Wrangell Museum
Cruise Ship Terminal
Front St
Swimming Pool
Hospital

Volunteer Park Trailhead

Bennett St

Church of God/ Roller Rink

Front St
Outer Dr
Kiksetti Totem Park
Wrangell Ave
Pine St
Zimovia Hwy
Etolin Ave

Tender Dock
City Hall
Case Ave

Chief Shakes V's Grave

Harbormaster Office/ Sea Plane Float Dock
Point Shekesti
Reliance Harbor
Chief Shakes Island
Inner Harbor
Case Ave
Ash St

WRANGELL

0   ¼   ½ Miles

0   ¼   ½   ¾ Kilometers

N
W   E
S

FAQs:

What do Alaskans mean by "Outside"?

This term, often uttered with a curled lip, indicates "the Lower 48"—that is, the rest of the United States. Because the Alaska Territory was ignored for decades after the Alaska Purchase, residents harbored considerable scorn for other Americans, and particularly for authorities far away in Washington, D.C. Aspects of this attitude linger, as in the bumper sticker, "We don't care how they do it Outside."

Do you accept U.S. currency?

As much as you can spare.

**How fast does the average
glacier move?**
In the Tongass, about an inch or two a
day—not fast enough to be seen with
the naked eye.

*Wrangell's history has been shaped by glaciers
and the Stikine River.*

followed the elder's lead, settling seven miles from the Stikine River delta, just south of modern Wrangell. The settlement was called Kots-lit-na (or Kotzlitzna) and the immigrant Tlingits became known as the Stikines (*stick-eens*).

As the glacier retreated, the Stikines used the river to trade with the Athabascans, exchanging goods such as fish oil and strings of dried clams for beaver and land-otter pelts. When the Russians arrived, they wanted control of the valuable Stikine trade. In 1833 emissaries of the Russian-American Company under Dionysius Fedorovich Zarembo began building Redoubt Saint Dionysius on what is now called Wrangell Island. (These rudimentary fortified outposts typically consisted of a trading post, a manager's house, and a barracks surrounded by a palisade of upright logs.) A scant six years later the discouraged Russians sold the outpost to the British, who renamed it Fort Stikine, and traded copper kettles, cloth, and Hudson's Bay Company blankets to the Stikine for furs. To keep an eye on things, the Stikine chief, one of seven named Shakes, moved his residence from Kots-lit-na 13 miles south to a small island in the harbor. The Tlingits did not favor the use of their traditional trade routes by

Visitors welcomed to Chief Shakes's home, ca. 1916.

Chief Toyatte Speaks

In the course of time a change came over the spirit of our dreams. We became aware of the fact that we were not the only beings in the shape of man that inhabited this earth. White men appeared before us on the surface of the great waters in large ships which we called canoes. Where they came from we knew not, but supposed that they dropped from the clouds. The ship's sails we took for wings, and concluded that, like the birds of the air, they could fly as well as swim. As time advanced, the white men who visited our country introduced among us every thing that is produced by nature and the arts of man. They also told us of a God, a superior being, who created all things, even us the Indians . . . and that all mankind were His children. . . . We are not the same people that we were a hundred years ago. . . .

. . . We have been told that the President of the United States has control over all the people, both whites and Indians. . . . He purchased this country from Russia, and in purchasing it he purchased us. We had no choice or say in change of masters. The change has been made and we are content. All we ask is justice.

. . . If you will all assist us in doing good and quit selling whisky, we will soon make Fort Wrangell a quiet place and the Stickeen Indians will become a happy people.

—Part of a speech by Chief Toyatte,
addressed to a packed schoolhouse at Wrangell, as transcribed by Presbyterian
missionary Amanda McFarland in 1877. From Polly and Leon Gordon Miller,
The Lost Heritage of Alaska: Adventures and Art of the Alaskan Coastal Indians, 1967

Hudson's Bay personnel. However, Native resistance became nominal after their population was reduced by half during smallpox epidemics in 1836 and 1840. Nevertheless, the British didn't last much longer here than the Russians, abandoning Fort Stikine in 1849.

In 1868, a year after America's Alaska Purchase, the trading settlement became a U.S. Army outpost called Fort Wrangell, named for Baron Ferdinand von Wrangel, chief manager for the Russian-American Company in the 1830s. Thus Wrangell became the only city in Alaska to have been governed by four nations.

Vincent Colyer, Special Indian Agent for the United States, visited Alaska in 1869. At Wrangell he observed 32 plank houses on a tongue of land, 500 yards from the government post "with the guns commanding the village." In front of Chief Shakes's house he noted three totem poles (today seen in replicas), describing them as "some very curious colossal frogs, a bear, war-chief, with his 'big medicine dance hat' on." Colyer here refers to Shakes V, also known as Wolf 18.

Over the next few years the U.S. Army tried to control uncooperative Alaska Natives through punishment. They "administered bombardments like righteous spankings," write art historians Polly and Leon Miller. Once, for example, a Kake and a Chilkat wanted to leave the village at Sitka to chop wood. A sentry shot them. In revenge, the Kakes killed two prospectors. General Jeff Davis then ordered the *Saginaw* to Kake Island, where it bombarded and destroyed the 16 houses of Old Kake and two other villages, plus canoes and food stored for winter. Some months later Wrangell was bombarded for various offenses—for one, a white laundress had had her finger bitten off.

For the most part, Wrangell was a sleepy little place until gold fever hit the interior. Strikes in the Cassiar District of British Columbia, 300 miles inland, brought a stampede of prospectors, all of whom needed provisions and tools—and most of whom sought recreation in saloons and brothels. In 1874 about 3,000 newcomers headed up the Stikine River to the Cassiar. By 1877 the army fort was abandoned as the soldiers were restationed Outside. Meanwhile, the three Stikine chiefs—Shakes V, Toyatte, and Shustaks—began requesting schools and churches. Their request was filled the following year by Presbyterian missionaries Amanda McFarland and S. Hall Young.

Naturalist John Muir went ashore at Wrangell in July 1879, and noted that about 1,800 miners were said to have passed through that season, about half of them Chinese. On one hand Muir criticized Wrangell as "a rough place" laid out with "devil-may-care abandon," but on the other he delighted in the profusion of wild berries, the community's affection for children, and the tranquility. "I never heard a noisy brawl in the streets or a clap of thunder," he wrote, "and the waves seldom spoke much above a whisper along the beach. . . . The cloudless days are calm, pearl-gray, and brooding in tone, inclining to rest and peace; the islands seem to drowse and float on the glassy water, and in the woods scarce a leaf stirs."

By 1880 steamers began running direct routes from Victoria, British Columbia, to Wrangell—but only every few weeks or so. Another wave of prospectors scrambled through in 1898 on their way to the Klondike in Canada's interior. Industry took root; two canneries and a sawmill opened, and a newspaper, the Wrangell *Sentinel,* began publishing in 1902.

Visitors steaming toward Wrangell in 1911 used Kodaks to record old totems and walked a wharf lined with Stikine Tlingit women selling baskets. In the yard

---

KID STUFF

- When the tide ebbs below the 12-foot level, treasure-hunt for the dozens of original petroglyphs on Petroglyph Beach. Cast-stone reproductions of several petroglyphs have been installed on the stairs to the beach so they can be viewed at high tide. Rubbings can be made of these casts—*not* the originals. (In years past, local children were allowed to make and sell petroglyph rubbings using ferns and rice paper. I'm proud to have their killer whale image hanging in my home.)

- The Wrangell Community Church of God (212 Bennett Street; skating rink, 907-874-2259) hosts a roller rink in its basement. Call for hours.

- The Irene Ingle Public Library (Second Street) offers computer games for kids as well as a cyber café. Check the *Sentinel* for gym hours and pick-up basketball games.

---

of the sawmill stood the abandoned plank house of Chief Kadashan, a man described by missionary Young as "the shrewdest and most diplomatic of the Stikeens . . . and a master of metaphors." Tourists hired a canoe to cross the slough separating the Native graveyard from Shakes Island. For half a dollar Shakes himself, 56, admitted visitors to his private museum and described the uses of the objects collected there. He also showed off his canoes and the 50-foot totem standing before his residence.

■ WRANGELL NOW *map page 48*

A loud exhalation sounds over the water. It draws the eye to blowhole mist a mile away. In a few seconds a humpback whale reveals the sleek curve of its back. More exhalations follow, almost like echoes. It's a pod of three females, one with her calf swimming close beside her, often sliding skin-to-skin against her for reassurance.

This scene is common near Wrangell and elsewhere along the Inside Passage. Humpbacks may travel in family groups of eight or more, sometimes blowing and feeding side by side like a marine chorus line. Today's visitors can record in their travel diaries many of the same vistas and species of wildlife that Muir and his friend Young recorded over a century ago.

Populations grow slowly in Southeast Alaska. In 1967 the Bureau of Indian Affairs counted a Wrangell city population of 1,500, including 1,000 Tlingits. By 2005 the town still had less than 3,000 people, but Natives now make up only

TOTEM POLES

Captain James Cook was one of the first Europeans to see and document the magnificent Northwest signpost, the totem pole. Unlike many other newcomers to the area, Cook was sensitive to Native art and did not condemn it outright as "pagan." He came close to the truth, surmising that totems were "images of some of their ancestors whom they venerate as divinities." It was hard to ignore totems 40 feet high, facing the shore as if to say "private property." Indeed those were the totems' messages. They reminded people of legends, of great chiefs, of clan lineage, and of claimed territory.

Totems are traditionally made from red cedar, using tools made of stone, shell, beaver tooth, and jade. The art of the totem reached its peak in the 1800s, when steel tools were introduced and the wealth from fur trading urged chiefs to compete in commissioning totems.

Traditional Tsimshian poles are known for their rhythm, sense of scale and proportion, precision, and sculptural technique. Details are rendered in low relief rather than by surface lines. Crests include the sea bear and whale. Color is used sparingly.

Haida poles use dramatic forms that overlap and interlock—forms cut deeply into the cedar but left unpainted. Haida crests include the seal, eagle, killer whale, and frog. Figures are static, as though freeze-framed.

Tlingit poles show a series of separated, superimposed, realistic forms. A watchman figure or clan crest may be placed at the top. Attached, projecting pieces such as an eagle's wings or a raven's beak are signature Tlingit devices. Figures are dynamic, portrayed climbing, sticking out a tongue, or flying. Color is used extensively—traditionally black, blue-green, red, and yellow. Paints were created from pulverized minerals or charcoal, with a fillip of fish eggs as a fixative.

One of the first important opportunities for Americans to see totem poles came with the Centennial Exhibition held in Philadelphia in 1876. Totems also drew visitors at the World's Columbian Exposition in Chicago in 1893. But by the late 1800s, as Native communities and folkways began to fray under the floods of prospectors, fox farmers, missionaries, and settlers, wood carving was on the decline. Missionaries often burned poles when tribes were away hunting or fishing, or they made converts demonstrate their conversion by burning poles and traditional regalia.

Public works projects in the 1930s and displays at the 1939 World's Fair helped to rekindle interest in totem poles, as did a carving workshop founded in Haines after World War II. Totems continue to be created today, usually on commission for a public building or in commemoration of a particular event.

Wrangell's mellow harbor.

roughly a quarter of the population. But because fewer cruise ships stop here, Wrangell doesn't get swallowed up by tourists in high season. It feels mellow and unhurried. At the ferry dock town children sell locally gathered garnets from muffin tins. The town's museum unlocks its doors only Tuesday through Saturday or when cruise ships and ferries are in port. Wrangell is still heralded as the "Gateway to the Stikine River," but no one seems in a rush to get there.

■ WALKING TOUR

Pick up a walking map at the **Wrangell Chamber of Commerce/Visitors Center** (110 Lynch Street; 907-874-3901 or 800-367-9745; www.wrangell.com) near the cruise-ship docks. The Wrangell Museum (2906 Outer Drive; 907-874-3770) shares a new building with the James & Elsie Nolan Civic Center. Expanded in 2004, the **Wrangell Museum** focuses on the town's history from prehistoric times through the missionary period. Note the photos of the original Shakes Tribal House and of Shakes VII at a 1940 potlatch. Of particular interest are four carved house posts dating from the late 1700s and thought to be the oldest Tlingit house posts in existence. There are also some lovely spruce-root and cedar-bark baskets

BASICS ON BEARS

The Inside Passage has thriving bear populations—both brown and black. Bears were some of the first large mammals to populate this vast wilderness after the ice sheets retreated. Remains of giant prehistoric bears in caves in Southeast Alaska have been carbon dated to 14,000 to 16,000 years ago, indicating that there were a few ice-free spots along the coast.

The brown bear, *Ursus arctos,* has thick fur that varies from dark chocolate-brown to blond as a showgirl. Also known as a grizzly, the brown bear is distinguished by a muscular hump at the shoulders, a dished face, and a large head. It is larger and has longer, straighter claws than the black bear. Coastal brownies with plenty of food in their habitat can grow to 1,400 pounds and stand over nine feet tall when they rise up out of tundra brush—a truly scary sight. Brown bears live on Admiralty, Baranof, and Chichagof islands as well as on the mainland.

Mature black bears average less than half the size of brownies—only 180 to 200 pounds. *Ursus americanus* is common all over North America. Black bears have short, curved claws and straight faces; their ears are bigger, and they're better at climbing trees than brownies. Like the brown bear, the black bear varies in color—from hematite-black to cinnamon-brown. There are 17,000 blackies concealed in Inside Passage forests. Those who venture from dense cover into human neighborhoods often develop a liking for the sweet syrup in hummingbird feeders, black-oil

A brown bear sow leads two cubs along the coast.

sunflower seeds, cracked corn, and dog kibble. In Juneau so many blackies raided downtown garbage that special bear-proof trash containers were installed in 2003.

The glacier or "blue" bear is a rare blue-gray color phase of the black bear. Its fur varies from a dirty white to black with many gray hairs and even overtones of green or silver. The first one was bagged near Yakutat in 1906, and few others have ever been seen.

Generally, black and brown bears do not mix in the same habitat. Both brown and black bears can swim, although neither can swim as well as the polar bear. Both have flattened molars for grinding plants such as roots, skunk cabbage shoots, angelica, berries, sedge on salt marshes, and beach grass. They fatten up in late summer, heading for favorite fishing streams. As snow begins to fall they den up, usually choosing a new den each year. For more information on bear sighting and safety tips, see the "Practical Information" chapter.

dating back to 1900. Trapping, fishing, and forest industries are represented in the collection. And don't fret; if you're in town on a Sunday or Monday the museum graciously opens by appointment.

Outside the museum, turn right on Front Street, pausing to examine the four totems at Kiksetti Totem Park. Front Street soon becomes Shakes Street, leading to the boardwalk to Shakes Island. Cross to the island to visit the **Tribal House of the Bear** (907-874-2023). This site is open based on cruise-ship dockings and by appointment. The tribal house is a 1939–40 replica of the original 1834 structure, erected with hand-adzed boards, without nails; the house posts are replicas of the four originals in the museum, carved without power tools. This setting is particularly moody if you see it in a heavy drizzle and are alone. Then the seven totems loom like giants in the gray mist, and you almost expect them to move. Two of them are replicas of totems carved in the late 1800s—totems that figure prominently in late-19th-century photo albums. The Bear-up-the-Mountain Totem with its unique bear footprints commemorates Shakes's ancestors and a grizzly who led them to safety on the highest ground in the area during a great flood. The Gonakadet Totem is a memorial pole, carved as a final resting place for the ashes of Chief Shakes VI's parents. Gonakadet is a legendary lake monster whose magic skin was stolen by a young man to satisfy his greedy mother-in-law.

Head back toward the dock, taking a right on St. Michael's Street and then a left on Church Street. The St. Rose of Lima Church (c. 1897) is the seat of

Alaska's oldest Roman Catholic parish. A little farther along, take a gander at the four Civilian Conservation Corps–carved totems on the grounds of the **Irene Ingle Public Library** (Second and Bevier streets). The CCC was a public works program in the 1930s.

For a vista of downtown, head up Bevier Street and take a right on Cassair Street. Climb the stairs leading to Third Street, which makes a couple of right turns to the **Mt. Dewey trailhead**. The hike to the top is quite easy; at 400 feet Mt. Dewey is hardly a mountain. After taking in the view, head back down to Second Street, turn right and then right again on Stikine Avenue, which parallels the shore of Zimovia Strait. About half a mile out of town stands an information kiosk at **Petroglyph Beach**, recently named a State Historic Park. The beach has one of the largest concentrations of petroglyphs along the Pacific Coast—about 40 of these ancient rock etchings. Look for spirals, big eyes, heart-shaped faces, and fish pecked into the faces of rocks facing seaward, near the high-tide line. No one knows how old the petrogylphs are, but they were apparently territorial signs for canoes exploring the beach. Those messages were probably sentiments like "This is our beach; no trespassing; catch your salmon elsewhere." Staff at the kiosk answer questions.

This entire walk will take three or four hours.

■ BRIEF EXCURSIONS

Want to stretch those hamstrings? **Rainwalker Expeditions** rents bikes and helmets. A 6-mile paved walking and biking path runs from downtown to the trailhead for Rainbow Falls at Shoemaker Bay. If you stay at Fennimore's B&B you can use a bicycle free (Second and Evergreen streets; 907-874-3012).

Take a hike. The **Rainbow Falls Trail**, just under a mile, is moderately steep. The 3½-mile **Institute Creek Trail** begins roughly half a mile up the Rainbow Falls Trail. Occasional muskeg (swamp) is bridged by boardwalks. You might see wildflowers like bog laurel and marsh marigold. There's a steep and muddy stretch, but persist and you'll be rewarded with Shoemaker Overlook, where you'll have panoramas of Zimovia Strait and Shoemaker Bay.

Wrangell offers the only USGA–rated golf course in Southeast Alaska. However, the 9-hole course, **Muskeg Meadows** (Ishiyama Road; 907-874-4653) has views of the ocean and mountain that may distract duffers from their game. Forgive me if I don't use phrases like "natural beauty" or "pristine wilderness" again, but trust me, it's here.

■ Longer Outings

Anan Creek Bear Observatory (800-367-9745) is one of the state's best places to see bears at close range from a relatively safe vantage point. Anan Creek is an ancient Tlingit fishing site with a large pink salmon run during July and August. Attracted by fat, juicy pinks and steelhead trout, black bears and the occasional brownie come to the creek to fish. (The fish draw seals, bald eagles, and ravens too.) The observatory is 35 miles south of Wrangell by plane or boat charter. You can view bears from an observation platform above the creek and a three-sided blind closer to the falls. Visitors are closely watched in turn by Forest Service personnel, who guide them along trails. No food is allowed on the trails or in the viewing areas, and flash photography is discouraged. Anan Creek is a very exclusive excursion. Only 64 visitors are allowed each day in July and August. Permits ($10) are available from the Forest Service office in Wrangell (907-874-2323). You can make it a day trip with Sunrise Aviation (800-874-2311; $99 per person) or take a boat trip that includes four hours at Anan. Don't expect the bears at rainy Anan to swat salmon out of the air like a circus act. The key things to have with you are good boots, rain gear, and patience.

Wrangell has 100 miles of forest roads to explore by hiking, mountain bike, or recreational vehicle. Pick up trail and mountain-bike information at the U.S. Forest Service Ranger Station (525 Bennett Street; 907-874-2323).

Follow the Stikine River into the **Stikine-LeConte Wilderness**. The wilderness has the world's second-largest concentration of eagles during spring spawning runs. The small, tasty, oily hooligan, which also run in spring, rate high on the food pyramid of gulls and Steller sea lions too. Moose, bears, and migrating waterfowl can also be viewed here, and from one spot on the river, you can see 21 glaciers. Breakaway Adventures (907-874-3455) offers all-day trips into the territory, with a stop at Chief Shakes Hot Springs for good measure. For something noisier, Alaska Waters (907-874-2378) offers jetboat trips up the Stikine. For kayaking or canoeing the Stikine, see the Forest Service guide available from the Wrangell Ranger District (907-874-2323).

Get a good look at migrating birds and other wildlife. Author, photographer, and former park ranger Karen Jettmar offers terrific outings with her **Equinox Wilderness Expeditions** (604-222-1219; www.equinoxexpeditions.com). These trips are timed to coincide with annual migrations; the nine-day Icy Bay expedition heads into Wrangell-St. Elias National Park.

PETERSBURG

If crowds are not your meat, pencil "Petersburg" into your travel planner. Today's supersized cruise ships are too broad in the beam to sail the channel leading to the town. Thus Petersburg currently sees only about 40,000 tourists a year. In fact, the town is so "out there" that it lacks home mail-delivery service. Nevertheless, it styles itself the "Heart of the Inside Passage."

Petersburg sits at the northern tip of Mitkof Island, a 211-square-mile chunk of real estate that's about 16½ miles wide at its widest point. The island's highest point is Crystal Mountain, at a mere 3,317 feet. Much of the island is soggy and low-lying—a muskeg, the northern term for what's called "swamp" in the Lower 48. Muskeg is a mossy wetland carpeted with plants such as heather, buckbean, and widely spaced, scraggly jack pines.

Mitkof Island is separated from Kupreanof Island by the 20-mile-long Wrangell Narrows. In fact, in some spots the Narrows are just wide enough to accommodate a state ferry. Confined in this channel, the tides slosh back and forth energetically, varying as much as 23 feet in a day. It's a thrilling ride, as you'll feel you can touch the banks on either side.

■ PETERSBURG THEN

Place names in the Petersburg area provide clues to its recent history. Duncan Canal, an inlet on Kupreanof Island, was named in 1793 by George Vancouver for an officer in the Royal Navy. Kupreanof Island, which forms the west shore of Wrangell Narrows, was named for Ivan Antonovich Kupreanof, the seventh chief manager of the Russian-American Company. Popular tourists destinations LeConte Bay and LeConte Glacier were named in 1887 for a geology professor at the University of California. Froot Loop Road is a 20th-century addition.

Tlingits maintained a fish camp here 2,000 years ago, and the abundance of fish also drew Norwegian immigrant Peter Buschmann to pick this as a spot for a cannery in 1897. Buschmann, an employee of Icy Straits Packing Company, soon had the surrounding glades ringing with the sound of pilings being driven for a wharf. In 1898 Buschmann installed a sawmill to churn out the lumber needed for the

The Leikarring Dancers of "Little Norway."

FAQs:

What is a "highliner"?
A skilled seine (net) fisherman, one who actually turns a profit.

What is "pulp" and what is made from it?
Straight logs are harvested to make boards, veneer, plywood, shingles, and shakes. (They are also called "mill" logs or "round" logs.) Crooked or damaged logs are harvested for pulp—the cellulose equivalent of mashed potato. This mash is processed into paper, cardboard, cellophane, photographic film, and synthetic fabrics such as rayon.

What is a rookery?
Usually the word means a breeding place or colony of European crows (rooks). In Alaska the word is used to describe

PETERSBURG

0   250   500 Feet

Alaska State Ferry route.
To Juneau

Blader St
First St
Charles St
High School
Swimming Pool
Dolphin St
Second St
Third St
Fifth St
Sandy Beach Rd
NorQuest Seafood Cannery
Excel St
Excel St
Cruise Ship Terminal
Petersburg Medical Center
Clausen Memorial Museum
Fourth St
Wrangell Narrows
North Boat Harbor
Fram St
Fram St
Visitor Information/ Chamber of Commerce
Way
Harbor
Chief John Lott St
Gjoa St
Gjoa St
To Airport, 1 mi.
Post Office
Viking Ship Replica
Forest Service Building
To
Falls Creek Fish Ladder, 9 mi.
Swan Observatory, 16 mi.
Crystal Lake Hatchery, 16.5 mi.
Three Lakes Loop Rd, 19 mi.
Haugen Dr
City Hall
Bojer-Wikan Fisherman's Memorial Park
Harbormaster Office/ Showers/Restrooms
Sons of Norway Hall
To
Ferry Dock, South Boat Harbor & Middle Boat Harbor
Ira II St
S Fourth St
Sing Lee Alley
Hammer's Slough
Birch St Boardwalk
Nordic Dr
Hammer's Slough Historical Area

Petersburg keeps close ties to its fishing-hub and Norwegian-immigrant past.

colonies or nesting groups of puffins, other gregarious sea birds such as kitti-wakes, or Steller sea lions. It is often a small, rocky, isolated island or cliff, preferred by birds because there are no predators (human or otherwise) to dis-turb their nests. If bald eagles try to nab nestlings they are "mobbed"—dri-ven off by a platoon of smaller birds, who cooperate on such occasions.

A replica Viking ship makes a perfect photo op.

cannery (completed in 1900). During its first season Icy Straits packed 32,750 cases of salmon. As the cannery flourished, summer-season workers decided to remain year-round. Homes and businesses sprang up around the cannery, many of them owned by Norwegians. A competitor, the Pacific Coast & Norway Packing Company, opened a saltery six miles south of Petersburg in 1900, and built a cannery the following year. On the strength of all this canning, Petersburg was incorporated in 1910. Six years later, NorQuest Seafoods built Alaska's first shrimp cannery at Petersburg. Tourists began arriving on a regular basis in 1912, when the Citizen Wharf Company built a dock and terminal for steamships.

■ PETERSBURG NOW *map page 65*

Norwegian was once commonly spoken along Petersburg's wooden streets, and the influence of Norway lingers. As you walk around town, you'll see blond braids, blue dirdles, ethnic sweaters, rosemaling (a type of decorative painting often applied to house fronts and shutters), and street names like "Gjoa." The Leikarring Dancers put on spirited performances at the Sons of Norway Hall.

Visit Hammer Slough at high tide to see the historic buildings reflected in the water.

There's a local taste for *lutefisk* (dried cod) and catered smorgasbords at weddings. For the Little Norway Festival on Syttende Mai (May 17, Norwegian Constitution Day) and again on July 4, locals pull out their old family recipes to make traditional Norwegian dishes such as *krumkake* (a crisp, waffle-like cookie rolled into a cylinder and filled with whipped cream) and *fattigmann* ("poor man's cake," a fried sweet pastry). All this Scandinavian atmosphere has earned the picturesque town the nickname "Little Norway."

As is true for the majority of Inside Passage communities, Petersburg doesn't lack for rain. The average annual precipitation is 110 inches, with half of that descending from October through December. To blend in with the 3,200 locals, just tug on a pair of X-tra Tuff boots and hitch your rain pants to rainbow suspenders.

Today Petersburg Medical Center is the town's largest employer, with federal, state, and local governments not far behind. Nevertheless, Petersburg remains a fishing town. Salmon is the main catch, but halibut, black cod, shrimp, herring, and crab (Dungeness, king, and tanner) are also strong fishery players. (Petersburg is also nicknamed the "halibut capital of Alaska.") Some fishermen are diversifying into geoduck, abalone, and sea cucumbers. Today the NorQuest Seafoods plant processes marine edibles ranging from shrimp and salmon to rockfish and sea urchins or "sea eggs." For fishing licenses or details about hooking onto a "barn door" (large halibut) yourself, head to the Alaska Department of Fish and Game (16 Sing Lee Alley; 907-772-3801). You can also get a fishing license from boat renters, fishing guides, and at grocery stores.

Petersburg-based activities include whale-watching in Frederick Sound or kayaking among the seals near LeConte Glacier (25 miles east). For details about humpback whale–watching, helicopter flightseeing, guided kayak tours, or glacier outings, consult Viking Travel (800-327-2571), Whale Song Cruises (907-772-9393), and Tongass Kayak Adventures (907-772-4600). More information is available from Petersburg Vacations (801 Odin Street; 877-442-4010). Because of the slower pace here, locals are happy to chat about the weather or flightseeing.

Anxious to check your e-mail? The Public Library, above the Fire Hall, offers free Internet access. The library is on Nordic Drive, between Haugen Drive and Birch Street.

■ WALKING TOUR

Cruise ships tie up at several locations—some at the south harbor near Sing Lee Alley; some at the fueling dock; and others in the north harbor. The town is so compact that there's no "main drag." Begin at the **Petersburg Visitor Information Center** (corner of First and Fram streets; 907-772-4636 or 866-484-4700; www. petersburg.org) for brochures and video presentations. Turn right on Fram Street, walking past the Medical Center to the **Clausen Memorial Museum** (203 Fram Street; 907-772-3598). Videos and demos by curators will show you how to catch a salmon or bait a crab pot. Displays illustrate the area's history with such artifacts as a 200-year-old Tlingit canoe from this region, carved yellow-cedar halibut hooks, and a stuffed 126½-pound king salmon caught in 1939. On the grounds, take a gander at the huge fish-trap anchors as well as the abstract aluminum *Fisk* sculpture by artist Carson Boysen. The museum is handicapped accessible.

Head back along Fram Street toward Wrangell Narrows, and turn left on Main Street/Nordic Drive. In a couple of blocks you'll reach **Hammer Slough**, where buildings perch on pilings above the water. At high tide the weathered structures are reflected in the Slough. At the entrance to the Slough is the **Sons of Norway Hall** (Sing Lee Alley; 907-772-4575), begun by Peter Buschmann in 1897. Decorated with rosemaling, the hall jumps during the Little Norway Festival and the King

OF FLIPPERS AND FLUKES

The Inside Passage's most common whale species are the humpback and the orca (killer whale). Whales are mammals; they're warm-blooded and breathe air. They're usually spotted when surfacing to exhale through blowholes on their backs. The exhale is full of water vapor, which can be seen from far off.

A humpback is a leviathan—45 to 50 feet long. Most of its body is dark gray, but its throat is creamy white. It has long pale flippers at its sides, and a huge, horizontal fluke or tail. When the fluke flips high into the air and shows itself in silhouette, the humpback is usually angling into the ocean for a long, deep dive.

Putting thousands of miles on their inner odometers, humpbacks migrate each year. They spend winter in the warm waters around the Hawaiian Islands or Baja, Mexico. Here female humpbacks give birth, and then as spring arrives, the whales migrate north to spend the summer in the feeding grounds off Alaska. The female humpbacks often swim in protective pods with their calves.

These enormous creatures feed on krill (tiny, shrimp-like organisms) and small fish. Humpbacks are baleen whales, so called for the series of fringed baleen plates that dangles from their upper jaws. The hair-like fringe acts as a strainer, separating food from sea water. Humpbacks may cooperate in a chorus line of six to eight, feeding side by side. Sometimes they "lunge feed"—plowing open-mouthed through concentrations of krill. Their most spectacular behavior is bubble-net feeding, in which they lunge up through the water, exhaling a curtain of bubbles which confuses and concentrates small fish. As the humpback reaches the surface, it explodes into the air, chasing the fleeing fish. Its pleated throat/belly expands as it gulps down its meal. Another signature humpback move is "breaching"—leaping into the air and slamming down on the water's surface. No one's sure why humpbacks breach; it could be a form of play. Humpbacks are also known for "singing." In winter, male humpbacks can emit complex patterns of sound for several hours at a stretch, while in summer they produce short tunes lasting only a minute or so.

The sleek, muscular orca, meanwhile, is a toothed whale with distinctive black and white markings. Orcas are usually about half the length of humpbacks, and they stay in the ocean off Alaska year-round. The orca is a powerful swimmer and can travel a hundred miles in a day. Males, known as bulls, have large dorsal fins up to six feet tall. The stiffness of the fin indicates the health of the whale.

Orcas generally travel in small pods and will hunt cooperatively, strategizing to capture prey and sharing their catches. Like humpbacks, orcas will spyhop and breach.

Drop by the Whale Observatory to look for passing humpbacks.

Salmon Derby, both in May. You might want to stop next door at Sing Lee Alley Books (907-772-4440) for its Alaskana. Near the hall is Bojer-Wikan Fisherman's Memorial Park, which commemorates local residents lost at sea. Birch Street Boardwalk parallels the Slough on one bank, with the Hammer Slough Historic Area on the other bank. For a taste of local entertainment, drop into **Kito's Kave** (Sing Lee Alley; 907-772-3207) for live music and Alaska-brewed beer.

Next, turn back to Nordic Drive and walk north several blocks to **Eagle's Roost Park**, where you'll have a good chance of seeing a bald eagle, especially in early summer. Continue on Nordic Drive to the Hungry Point View Area, which has views of the Coast Mountains and the peak of Devil's Thumb. Here Nordic Drive becomes Sandy Beach Road. You can turn onto Hungry Point Trail, a 40-minute walk where black-tailed deer hang out. The trail will lead you back to town. Or you may choose to walk farther on Sandy Beach Road to the beach access at

KID STUFF

■ First, buy a horned Viking hat at Kinder Komfort (Sing Lee Alley; 907-772-4100). Then head to Bojer-Wikan Fisherman's Memorial Park and climb aboard the *Valhalla*. With its striped sail and fiddlehead prow, the model ship provides a cute photo op.

■ Sign up for a rosemaling class at the Cubby Hole (102 South Second Street; 907-772-2717). Rosemaling is a Norwegian decorative art of painted or carved floral designs; it translates as "rose painting." The classes are geared to all ages, and you usually paint on wood.

■ Kids under 12 can fish off the dock without a fishing license. It's possible to catch herring or Dolly Varden.

■ For a chance at a $2,000 first prize, guess how many one-pound cans of salmon will be packed in Petersburg in the current season. Tickets are sold July 1 to August 21 at 907-772-4294; the winner is announced during Seafood Fest in October.

■ Hike to Fisheries Hill and Eagle's Roost Park, where bald eagles perch as they watch for fish in Wrangell Narrows. Another good spot for viewing eagles is Hungry Point, where many nest. Bring binoculars to spy on nestlings without disturbing them.

the **Whale Observatory**. Here mounted binoculars help you scan the ocean for flukes and spouts, and interpretive signs provide info on marine mammals such as humpbacks and orcas.

This walk will take several hours—or most of a day, depending on how long you spend in the museum, bookstore, park, or bar.

■ BRIEF EXCURSIONS

Bird-watch at the **Swan Observatory** (Mile 16, Mitkof Highway, no phone), a shielded place from which to view trumpeter swans. Dozens of these large, beautiful waterfowl spend the winter on Mitkof Island, and hundreds more take a break here between mid-October and early December while migrating south. In summer, bears and salmon splash in the shallow water downriver from the observatory.

If you're archaeologically curious, sign up for a tour with a U.S. Forest Service guide to see petroglyphs and prehistoric Tlingit fish traps on **Sandy Beach**. The

Walking, Wading, Climbing, Slithering

The small island was an unlimited world. I was never bored. It was a thrill just walking in the woods, for the aimless jaunts always seemed to lead to discoveries. I was forever learning something new about nature or myself. Both I came to realize as being one and the same. The external world reflects our internal composition: a circulatory system of streams and rivers, a sensitive skin of earth, mountain spines, stones as bones, breathing in the surf, hair on grassy headlands. The Indians regarded the earth as a living entity—a human system on a grand scale. And the resemblance went as far as psychological forces finding release as birds, trees, whales, and the weather. As Gary Snyder wrote, "Outwardly, the equivalent of the subconscious is the wilderness."

. . .To make my way, I walked, waded, climbed, and now dropped to hands and knees, or in tight spots slithered through on my belly. As I went further in, I saw cedar trees that had grown immense, nearly as giant as their redwood cousins. Overhead, their broad canopies closed out sunlight. . . .

The high tree needles and leaves tapered to points that pierced the rain. Water fell in long drops, penetrating deep into mossy beds. Gurgling rivulets of water cut channels through the layered loam. Even the rocks looked as soft and porous as sponges. The air was rich with decay. The smell wasn't putrid but had a clean yeasty odor that expanded in the lungs.

—Michael Modzelewski, *Inside Passage: Living with Killer Whales, Bald Eagles, and Kwakiutl Indians*, 1991

petroglyphs, showing heart-shaped faces with circular eyes and mouths, are on a large rock outcrop. Nearby, visible at low tide, are the remains of five heart-shaped wood-stake fish traps. The oldest traps are two stone structures—one on either side of the beach—which are nearly 3,000 years old. Over 30 feet across, the traps led fish at high tide into a maze of two overlapping circles. As the tide ebbed, fish were caught in the maze. Tlingits could then spear the fish or gather them by hand. You can also see remnants of five later traps fashioned from hemlock stakes pounded into the sand—a type of fish trap found nowhere else in the world.

(left) Cathy Harris, owner of the Cubby Hole, demonstrates rosemaling.
(following pages) You'll have a good chance of seeing bald eagles at Eagle's Roost Park.

These are about 2,000 years old. The Forest Service shares an office with the Visitor Information Center (corner of First and Fram streets; 907-772-4636).

Interested in an introduction to a noisy, gooey "slime line"? Cannery tours supply an up-close look at fish processing. **Tonka Seafoods** offers hour-long tours (22 Sing Lee Alley; 888-560-3662; www.tonkaseafoods.com). The forces of fish and bleach do battle at fish processing plants, providing a damp but not unpleasant milieu. Tonka is a small, intimate operation; on a big day they process 2,000 pounds. The owners act as tour guides, explaining the basics of the seafood industry, and then taking you into the main work room where you see fish beheaded and gutted. Samples are distributed at the close of the tour.

If you're interested in fish raising instead, head out to **Crystal Lake Fish Hatchery** (Mile 17, Mitkof Highway; 907-772-4772). The hatchery raises 1.5 million king salmon and 150,000 cohos. Most are released right there, although some are taken to Anita Bay near Wrangell and some to Neets Bay outside Ketchikan. A visit here is a do-it-yourself excursion—you can walk around 24 outdoor tanks called "raceways." It's fun to watch when food pellets are tossed over the surface of the raceways and the water boils in feeding frenzy. The most exciting time to visit is July and August, when adult cohos return and can be seen through glass windows in the fish ladder.

Tonka Seafoods can introduce you to a "slime line."

Take a stroll along the **Blind River Rapids Trail**, 14 miles from downtown off the Mitkof Highway. A quarter-mile boardwalk leads to the rapids, passing over a muskeg. It's an easy half-hour walk, but you may want to linger for several hours because this spot offers one of the few opportunities in the Inside Passage to fish from shore for king salmon during June and July. (The visitors center has a complete list of local outfitters.) The boardwalk is handicapped accessible, as are restrooms and a shelter at trail's end.

Fly over **LeConte Glacier**, which squats on the mainland between town and the Stikine River. It's the southernmost active tidewater glacier in North America, often calving bergs into the 15-mile-long fjord named Frederick Sound. Occasionally bergs float onto Petersburg beaches or into the boat harbors. LeConte's icefield has shrunk about 100 feet since a 1948 aerial survey. For flightseeing, contact Kupreanof Flying Service (907-772-3396). From above, glaciers are sinuous extrusions ribbed by rock debris and pocked with deep crevasses. Flights last about 45 minutes. Weather is tricky here, so you shouldn't urge a pilot to take off if he or she is reluctant. Charter boats also offer sightseeing trips to Frederick Sound.

■ LONGER OUTINGS

Petersburg is a doorway to the **Tongass National Forest**. The Petersburg Ranger District maintains 20 recreation cabins. Most of the cabins are accessible by boat or floatplane only, making them ideal for soaking up the solitude of remote wilderness. The Mallard Slough cabin near LeConte Bay can be reserved by applying at the Petersburg Ranger District front desk, through the National Recreation Reservation Service (877-444-6777; www.reserveusa.com).

There are no Forest Service cabins in LeConte Bay, but the Ranger District provides a cabin that meets barrier-free standards: the Kah Sheets Lake Cabin. It can be reached by way of a 2½-mile boardwalk from Kah Sheets Bay. A rowboat is provided for sockeye fishing.

Listen to humpback whales sing on a cabin-cruiser trip with Captain Ron Loesch of **Whale Song Cruises**. On a six-hour trip you can use a hydrophone, which magnifies underwater sounds, to hear the haunting whale calls. Loesch also offers wildlife viewing, transportation to cabins, fishing, and sightseeing (907-772-9393; www.whalesongcruises.com).

Take a week-long guided kayak tour of the Tongass with **Tongass Kayak Adventures** (907-772-4600; www.tongasskayak.com). This isn't a marathon paddling situation, but you should be in good shape. You'll take kayaking day trips out of a fixed camp, poking around and seeing cool stuff like icebergs and waterfalls in crannies of LeConte Bay. All guides are naturalists.

J   U   N   E   A   U

Juneau has a magnificent setting, most dazzling on a clear evening when its lights twinkle. It lies on the inland side of Gastineau Channel. Viewed from the harbor, two precipitous, deeply gullied mountains seem to rise directly from the shallow cup that holds downtown. These mounts are Juneau and Roberts. In summer the harbor is further brightened with strings of lights looped between smokestacks of cruise ships.

Juneau lies near the head of navigation for Gastineau Channel, as, at low tide, the flat coming from either shore leaves only a shallow channel for two miles. Cruise ships penetrating the eight miles into the Channel from Stephens Passage must perform a 180° turn to exit. Forming the far side of the channel at Juneau's door is Douglas Island. Douglas is a mountainous 20 miles long. The foothills facing downtown Juneau house bedroom communities and Eaglecrest Ski Area. Wolves and Sitka deer live in its forests. The deer are a tiny species—perfect for making a malamute drool.

The city is often swathed in climbing mists, with the occasional pea-souper. Even in August, cruise ships approaching via Gastineau Channel sometimes need to sound their fog horns. Juneauites spend many a day in the knee-high rubber boots otherwise know as "Southeast sneakers."

■ JUNEAU THEN

According to Tlingit oral history, the first humans here were the Auk-Kwaan, "lake people." Precisely dating the arrival of Tlingits is impossible. However, a fish trap discovered in the muddy bank of Montana Creek in 1991 gives important clues. The 700-year-old trap, woven of hemlock and spruce, is the oldest artifact ever found in the Juneau area. Oral tradition holds that the Tlingit migrated here 8,000 to 10,000 years ago.

The Auk and Taku Tlingit followed a seasonal round of food-gathering activities. The Auk, for example, had a fish camp on Gastineau Channel when fish were running. The breezes at this site helped dry the fish. In winter they retreated to a more sheltered village near Auk Lake.

Get a lift (and a great view) from the Mount Roberts Tramway.

Misty, rainy Juneau is sometimes called the "Gateway to the Glaciers."

FAQs:

How far are we above sea level?

Juneau is tucked in the back pocket of Gastineau Channel. A century ago, South Franklin Street and Willoughby Avenue were beach where Auk Tlingits pulled their canoes above high tide line. Gradually through the 1920s and '30s, mine tailings created new land. So unless you hike up Mt. Roberts, you're just a few feet above sea level most of the time.

With 222 days of mist and rain, why don't Juneauites use umbrellas?

They go by the drip-dry principle.

Can I drive to Juneau?

Nope. Juneau is the only one of the 50 U.S. capitals that is not connected to the rest of the state's road system. Take a plane or load your vehicle on a ferry. The Alaska Department of Transportation is studying the possibility of a road to Skagway, but hundreds of avalanche chutes and bald eagle nesting sites are in the way. In addition, only half the population of Juneau supports the idea—and much of Skagway opposes it.

How much of Juneau is under ice?

A century ago, big bergs calved from Mendenhall Glacier regularly floated past downtown. But don't pack an ice axe. Global warming has nipped those bergs in the bud. The Juneau Ice Field is North America's fifth largest—it's larger than Rhode Island. The ice field spawned Juneau's nickname, "Gateway to the Glaciers."

GREATER JUNEAU

Mendenhall Lake

Mendenhall Glacier

Mendenhall Glacier Visitors Center

Mendenhall Loop Rd

MENDENHALL VALLEY

Mendenhall River

Glacier Spur Hwy

Mendenhall Loop Rd

Mendenhall

Egan Dr

To Auke Bay Ferry Terminal

Terminal

Raptor Center

Bartlett Hospital

Drive

Macaulay Salmon Hatchery

Juneau International Airport

Mendenhall Wetlands State Game Refuge

Tongass National Forest

North Douglas Highway

Gastineau Channel

SALMON CREEK

Egan Drive

Salmon Creek

Tongass National Forest

DOUGLAS ISLAND

Mt Juneau 3,576

Last Chance Basin

Basin Rd

Gold Creek

Downtown Juneau See map p84

Juneau-Douglas High School

WEST JUNEAU

To Eaglecrest Ski Area, 12.2 mi.

DOUGLAS

JUNEAU

Cruise Ship Terminal

Mt Roberts

To Historic Gold Mine Town & Thane

Prospectors drawn by Juneau's gold strike, early 20th century.

This subsistence lifestyle continued undisturbed for centuries. Eventually, however, Western explorers began to probe the nearby waterways as they sought a rumored Northwest Passage that would connect the Pacific with the Atlantic. The Spanish explored near here in 1779. Then came various British expeditions. At the same time, Russians were gradually establishing settlements as they fanned out from bases to the north and west at Unalaska, Kodiak, Kenai, and Prince William Sound.

Often the Tlingit did not greet these newcomers with open arms. For instance, as the British lieutenant Joseph Whidby explored Lynn Canal for Captain George Vancouver in July 1794, a large canoe approached bearing a chief who made Whidby a present of a sea-otter skin. The chief was magnificently dressed in a Chilkat blanket and a copper and brass "crown" from which ermine skins dangled. The following day several other British canoes arrived, and the chief's attitude became less cordial. He attempted to board the yawl, apparently to plunder it. Whidby escaped from these Natives—probably Auks—and came to a place which Vancouver named Berners Bay, 40 miles from modern Juneau's downtown. As they navigated Favorite Channel, they saw smoke and Tlingit in various directions; in Gastineau Channel Natives threatened them again.

Tracing Juneau's Gold Belt

Juneau's Gold Belt is an ore-rich corridor stretching from Dupont to Eagle River. With the help of wooden footbridges, gravel trails, and the occasional cable set into the rock face, you can trace the paths of miners all along this corridor.

One of the most accessible remnants of Juneau's mining past is **Basin Road**. You can reach it from the top of Gold Street; it hugs the lower slopes of Mt. Roberts. While on this road you'll hear the rush of Gold Creek in its canyon below, and catch glimpses of it from the massive wooden trestle bridge that leads into Last Chance Basin and Silver Bow Basin—the sites of Joe Juneau and Dick Harris's gold discoveries in 1880.

Along Basin Road you'll come to the Last Chance Mining Museum, clinging to the slope of Last Chance Basin (*see* Brief Excursions). This area once had a boarding house, bunkhouses, machine shops, and train sheds. Five hundred men labored in three shifts on the fifteen levels of Mt. Roberts during the peak years of activity (1915–35). Tunnels through the mountain connected this spot to the mill where the ore was processed; the skeleton of the mill can be seen on the slopes above downtown Juneau.

Just above the parking lot for the mining museum, at the first curve of **Perseverance Trail**, stands a shaft entrance. If you step into the entry you'll feel a blast of subterranean cold from the blocked tunnel. Imagine laboring in this ice box for eight hours at a stretch. The hike up Perseverance Trail, following the route of an old wagon road, is an easy climb. The trail is popular with joggers, but note that it is disintegrating on the downhill side.

For hikers who don't want to attempt Perseverance, **the flume** offers a more level walk. Accessed from a small parking lot at the end of Evergreen Avenue, the flume is a mile-long, boxed water trough. Once the flume carried water to create power for mining; today it carries part of the city's drinking water. Handrails and planking atop the wooden trough act as a boardwalk from the end of Evergreen Avenue to the first bridge on Basin Road. This elevated perch offers good views of rock slides and glimpses into the spruce and hemlock forest. Goat's beard, currants, stinging nettles, and the thorny devil's club flourish along the flume.

For another view of mining history, seek out the **Treadwell Historic Trail** on Douglas Island (*see* the Treadwell Past and Present sidebar).

DOWNTOWN
JUNEAU

After circumnavigating Admiralty Island (on the far side of Douglas Island), Whidby explored Taku Inlet. His passage was blocked by bergs. The basin at the end seemed sheathed in ice and the mountains wrapped in perpetual snow. He could find no place to land. Because of these negative early impressions and Auk Tlingit threats, it took nearly a century for newcomers to establish a foothold here.

Gold Creek, which winds its chilly course through downtown Juneau, was once a Tlingit fishing-camp site. The Tlingit called the creek *Dzantik'i Heeni,* or "where the flounder/flatfish gather." In autumn 1880 a local Aak'w (or Auk) Tlingit chief, Kowee, led two Canadian prospectors to the creek mouth. Kowee was anxious to earn a reward offered by a Sitka mining engineer: 100 wool blankets plus day labor for his tribe. The prospectors, Joe Juneau and Richard Harris, frittered away their

The Amalgam Thieves

At the Treadwell mines, gold was crushed from the ore in the stamps. This gold was amalgamated with mercury in the stamp block. The gold-laden mercury, called amalgam, was then heated, causing the mercury to vaporize and leave pure gold. For several years prior to 1905, Supt. Kinzie had been disturbed because of a discrepancy between away values or ore going into the mill and the gold recovered in the clean-ups. The assays consistently indicated that more gold should have been recovered. . . .

Kinzie had hired the "cleverest Pinkerton detective in the west" who quickly noticed that Mrs. Mary Freestone made regular trips to Seattle. He followed her on one trip, and, in Seattle Mrs. Freestone went directly to an assay office where she deposited a retort full of gold under the name of C.T. Arthur.

The detective promptly had Mrs. Freestone arrested. The shock of the arrest "nearly prostrated" the woman and she confessed completely. It seemed that her husband would steal small portions of the amalgam, take it home and retort it there.

Mr. Freestone was arrested, and, when told of his wife's confession, broke down and freely admitted his crime. What had started as a small theft continued until a substantial amount of amalgam had been taken, from which about $3,400 of gold was retrieved by the Freestones.

—Earl Redman, *History of the Mines and Miners in the Juneau Gold Belt*, 1988

time on their first trip. However, on a second trip that year Kowee guided them up the creek into a high plateau called Bear's Nest (now Silver Bow Basin). The pair was ecstatic to find "large pieces of quartz spangled over with gold . . . little lumps as large as peas and beans." News of the strike spread quickly, and by the close of the year 30 miners were in residence. At first the town was called Harrisburgh, then Rockwell, and finally Juneau City—after Joe reputedly bought several rounds of drinks. By the following winter Juneau had a blacksmith shop, 150 miners, and 450 Tlingits.

Juneau forms the "buckle" of a mineralized district known as the Juneau Gold Belt. This district extends from Windham Bay north to the head of Lynn Canal, about 120 miles total. A Geological Survey bulletin of 1906 notes, "In whatever

(following pages) The Lynn Canal, one of the gateways to Juneau.

direction one travels from Juneau within this belt, quartz mines are to be found in every stage, from the prospect to the highly developed mines." Gold mining held steady until World War II. Juneau was known for its mining innovations. As Juneau historian David Stone, author of *Hard Rock Gold*, recounts, the mines offered stock options, eight-hour shifts, and workmen's comp before these benefits were implemented anywhere else in the world.

From the 1830s on, Tlingit populations were devastated by a series of epidemics. Most surviving Natives lost faith in their traditions and sought Western schooling and religion. Meanwhile, tourists judged the area safe for travel. They visited mines, haggled for baskets, and returned home with gold-nugget watch chains galore. Taku Glacier, which had discouraged Whidby, became a popular pause on cruise routes. As a result, steamships began delivering tourists to Juneau's Steamship Dock (now the Cruise Ship Terminal Dock) in 1884. Early sightseers interested in mining sought out the Treadwell properties on Douglas Island.

In 1906 the capital of Alaska was transferred from Sitka to Juneau, partially because Juneau's economic star was rising. The contrast between Sitka and Juneau is perhaps best expressed by Hannah Breece, who taught school in Alaska between 1904 and 1918. She passed through both ports in the summer of 1912 on her way to a teaching post at Fort Yukon. She found Sitka charming and quaint, "like a dear and proper old lady dozing in her chair. Juneau was like a strapping young fellow striding to his work."

The economy of Southeast Alaska has been described as a "three-legged stool" of fisheries, pulp mills, and tourism. As the state capital, Juneau has a fourth leg: the state legislature, whose 120-day sessions begin in January. Since the 1970s, voters in Anchorage have lobbied to move the capital closer to their doorstep, since half of Alaska's population now resides in or near Anchorage. Factions continue to push and shove on the issue—some mumbling "something's gotta give," while others support Juneau with righteous indignation.

■ **JUNEAU NOW** *map pages 81 and 84*

Visitors may pigeonhole Juneau as a jumping-off spot for magnificence like Glacier Bay, 50 miles to the northwest. But Juneau is a destination in its own right. Downtown has a handful of glass-and-concrete highrises (including one called the "Spam Can"), but it's no Manhattan. Just blocks from the downtown are Queen Anne–style homes and tiny miners' shacks. A dozen miles away the Mendenhall

LIGHTHOUSES

A dozen lighthouses stand guard on or near the dangerous rocks and reefs of the Inside Passage. Needed for safe navigation in the passage's tricky waters, especially in dense fog or whiteout conditions, their lights warn ships to steer clear of hazards.

As you sail north, the lighthouses along the route include Tree Point at Dixon Entrance; Mary Island in Revillagigedo Channel; Cape Decision on Sumner Strait; Five Fingers in Stephens Passage; Point Retreat, Sentinel Island, and Eldred Rock in Lynn Canal near Juneau; and Cape Spencer in Cross Sound.

These lighthouses were once manned by keepers who filled the lamps with seal or whale oil and polished the big lenses which helped magnify the light. Today, however, all lights are fully automated, powered by solar batteries. Some are being restored by local historical societies; some can be rented. In 2004 Juneau installed informational plaques about Alaska's lighthouses along Steamship Dock Wharf.

In addition to lighthouses, the Inside Passage has navigational aids such as red and green buoys, lighted buoys, and blinking signals. Signs on shore warn of underwater cables or other hazards. Wrangell Narrows is so dangerous that more than 70 navigational markers guide ships along the 21 miles between Wrangell and Petersburg—there are so many lights that Alaskans have nicknamed this passage "Christmas Tree Lane."

Valley presents woodsy, quiet residential streets resembling exterior shots from "Father Knows Best." Juneau has several hubs, including the downtown waterfront and business district; the headquarters of the 17th Coast Guard on Egan Drive; residences and schools near 12th Street; a handful of small boat harbors; "the Valley"; and the University of Alaska Southeast. Each area has its fan club.

There's a saying in the Last Frontier that its cities are "only 20 minutes from Alaska." That means that wilderness is a short distance from the busiest thoroughfare. This juxtaposition is particularly striking in Juneau, where black bears amble through perennial beds so often that black-oil sunflower seeds in bird feeders are discouraged.

Walk toward Mount Juneau from downtown in June and you'll soon hear a low thrumming issuing from the forested slopes. It's the mating song of the male blue grouse. Crows kibitz from the branches of mountain ash, making sounds like rakes on concrete. Occasionally they imitate cats. The "ringing telephone" is the varied thrush—a black and orange songster slightly larger than a robin.

North of town, the Mendenhall is Juneau's "drive-up" glacier. The Mendenhall is retreating, meaning it melts faster at its snout or terminus than it grows at its source. The Taku Glacier is advancing, with more ice added by snowfall at its source than it loses from melting. Both are part of the Juneau Ice Field, as are the Herbert and Eagle glaciers "out the road." (Juneau's "road system" is minor arteries plus a 20-mile long highway headed north. Anything along the highway is called "out the road.") South of town, Taku Glacier is a popular site, but cannot be accessed by road.

The gold-mining past has been a boon to hikers, as many of the city's most popular hiking routes are old mining trails. But in fact, gold mining may not be just history. Juneau's three largest hard-rock gold mines (the Treadwell Complex, the Alaska Gastineau, and the Alaska-Juneau or A-J) eventually produced 7 million ounces of gold—about $3 billion in 2004 values. With the price of gold continuing to rise, new mines are being considered for the Taku River (over the border in Canada) and in Berners Bay, north of Juneau.

■ WALKING TOURS

Juneau offers so much to see that one walking tour of it all would exhaust most visitors. Below, I've broken up sightseeing walks according to themes of interest. Each of these walks will take one to two hours.

■ HISTORIC DOWNTOWN JUNEAU

Many of the original buildings built in the 1880s and 1890s still stand. Within a seven-block radius there are 60 buildings built before 1904. Eleven are listed on the National Register of Historic Places; just a few are open to the public. Some, like the Alaska Steam Laundry (174 South Franklin; 1901, now a mall) are not particularly impressive, but others are quite eye-catching.

Start at the three-story **Alaskan Hotel & Bar** (167 South Franklin; 907-586-1000). This is Juneau's oldest continuously operating hotel. When the Alaskan's doors opened on September 16, 1913, champagne flowed, two bands played, and free ferries brought guests over from Douglas. The hotel was cutting-edge at the time, because it featured steam heat and a wireless station of 1.5 kilowatts on the roof. A window flanking the front door retains its Tiffany stained glass. The current owners, Mike and Bettye Adams, have renovated the 30 rooms with antique oak furniture.

Next, turn right and continue up South Franklin. At 229 North Franklin, take in the 1904 **William Winn/Bell House.** Its style is "Juneau eclectic," meaning it began as a no-nonsense residence/boardinghouse but took on airs in 1986 when Queen Anne gingerbread and "painted lady" hues were added. Robert Stroud, the pimp who became famous as "the Birdman of Alcatraz," is said to have boarded here. The house is just a block and half from the spot where, in 1909, Stroud violently murdered a bartender he thought had cheated him.

If you want to see the **Alaska State Capitol** (Seward and Fourth streets; 907-465-2479), make a detour left on Fourth Street. On summer weekdays you can take a free guided tour. The pillared building (1929–31) is used by the legislature January through May.

Continue uphill, taking a right on Fifth Street. The **St. Nicholas Russian Orthodox Church** (326 Fifth Street; 907-586-6790) has a dramatic setting, with the rock-slide scars and dark forest of Mt. Juneau rising behind it. The church (1897) is the oldest unaltered church in Southeast Alaska. It was either constructed on site—or built in Russia, disassembled, and sent here. No one is quite sure. But its octagonal shape and gold onion dome make it a favorite with photographers and painters. The interior is a gilded jewelbox decorated with icons and artwork, some dating from the 18th century. You're welcome to attend an incense-scented service, held in the church language of Slavic, but custom dictates one stands throughout. The bookstore/gift shop adjoining is even larger than the church.

From the church, climb up Gold Street to Sixth Street, then hang a left. Pause on the left-hand side of the street to take in **The Family**, a three-part totem carved by local artist Michael Beasley in 1996. Next, take a right onto the second staircase you come to.

A snowy day in downtown Juneau.

ROOTS TRAVEL: FINDING GREAT-GRANDDAD

Are you looking for Great Granddad, the mysterious missing miner? If so, you'll find excellent resources in the Inside Passage. Some of the 100,000 stampeders who headed for Alaska and the Yukon during the Klondike Gold Rush traveled under assumed names. Some disappeared. Others hunkered down at remote creeks and never wrote home. But if there are any traces of them, you have a good shot of finding them here.

Cemeteries might give you a lead, such as the Gold Rush Cemetery in Skagway. Most graves there date from 1898 to 1904.

Instead of reading headstones, you could search through turn-of-the-20th-century documents. Visit the Skagway Museum & Archive (Seventh and Spring streets, P. O. Box 521, Skagway 99804; 907-983-2420). The Archive keeps records of persons crossing the Canadian border during the Stampede years, plus additional details from logs kept by the Royal Canadian Mounted Police. The archive also houses passenger lists from the White Pass Steamship Line and Skagway and Dawson prison files.

The Juneau-Douglas City Museum (Fourth and Main streets; 907-586-3572) is a treasure trove for amateur genealogists. "Many prospectors looking for gold in Alaska came through Juneau," notes Ellen Carrlee, Curator of Collections. "If relatives have a range of years when they suspect an ancestor was here, that's helpful. A full name with middle initial and names of partners or wives are also useful in tracing people. There are lots of places where people had to register. If they collected Social Security here, or ran for office, those records may show birth date, death date, and place of death." The museum maintains an index of employees of the Alaska-Juneau Mine (1897–44) and its shop sells copies of historical studies and limited-edition references.

The Alaska State Library in Juneau has prepared an "Alaska Genealogy Resource Guide," which lists dozens of resources available to researchers. Copies of this six-page brochure can be found on its Web site, www.library.state.ak.us. The Alaska State Archives, located downstairs from the Alaska State Library at 141 Willoughby Street, stores records, probate documents, and court records (907-465-2270; www.archives.state.ak.us/).

For Internet research, try the Yukon & Alaska Genealogy Centre in Whitehorse site, www.yukonalaska.com/pathfinder/gen/, which allows access to information assembled by Pathfinder Publications and others. Sample databases include an index to proprietors and managers of historic Alaska and Yukon hotels, wayhouses, saloons, and cafes, and a list of the 203 families in the Matanuska Colony.

A CMT (culturally modified tree) on Mt. Roberts.

Tucked into the corner formed by this staircase and Sixth Street is the J.M. Davis House, the residence of Frances Brooks, a British painter who moved to Juneau in 1891, and J. Montgomery Davis, whom she married in 1892. As you climb, there are clear views of its gardens of foxgloves, daisies, columbine, and rugosa roses. You'll also get glimpses into other terraced gardens. At the top is Chicken Ridge— named for the ptarmigan that early miners bagged here. To your right stands the **Hammond-Wickersham House** (213 Seventh Street; 907-586-9001), a mansion built in 1899 for the superintendent of the Sheep Creek Mine. Its most famous resident was Judge James Wickersham, politician and author, who bought the house in 1928. This house is occasionally open; call for availability. To see the judge's view from his glassed-in porch, walk onto the lawn and turn toward the Channel.

From the Wickersham House, turn left on Seventh Street. Pause at its intersection with Main Street for a San Francisco–like view down the steep street to the steamship wharf. If you descend Main for three blocks, you're back at the State Capitol and the City Museum.

■ Animals

For a great photo op, climb on the **Windfall Fisherman** on Seward Street in front of the Dimond Courthouse. The life-size bronze of a grizzly content with his catch was designed by R.T. Wallen, a sculptor who knows his bear anatomy well. Juneau's most famous animal statue is **Patsy Ann**, posed alertly on the steamship wharf at Marine Park. Patsy Ann (1929–42) was a deaf bull terrier who "heard" the whistles of approaching ships and faithfully met vessels as they tied up at this wharf. You can find animals of another kind at the downtown hangouts on Front Street, like the Viking Bar and the Imperial.

■ Totem Poles and Local Artifacts

Juneau's **totem poles** may not be tidily grouped together in a park, but they're well worth seeking out. There were 20 poles at last count. Downtown examples include Amos Wallace's Harnessing the Atom Totem near the City Museum on Calhoun Street. The venerable Waasgo or Old Witch Pole, in the lobby of the State Office Building at Fourth and Calhoun streets, was carved by Dwight Wallace in 1880 for the Quit-aas clan at Sukwan. Old Witch was originally moved to Juneau to lure customers to a souvenir shop, then moved indoors in 1977. Almost no poles of this vintage remain in existence, so the Old Witch is a rare bird indeed. Juneau's newest totem is a sinuous, unpainted pole in the foyer of the Mt. Roberts Tramway at the cruise-ship dock.

Pore over the relief map of Juneau in 1967 at the **Juneau-Douglas City Museum** (Fourth and Main streets; 907-586-3572). The detailed map was created by a high school student using aerial photos and contour maps, to a scale of 1 inch to 1,320 feet (or 4 inches to the mile). A pull-out step helps kids get a good look. Another draw is the remains of a basketry fish trap excavated from Montana Creek in 1991. The trap, about 700 years old, went on exhibit in 2005, and has a full-size model suspended above it, plus hands-on supplemental materials.

■ The Governor's House and the Waterfront

Tailings (waste rock) from the Alaska-Juneau Mine were laid down to create much of Juneau's modern waterfront, including the flat land where Egan Drive now stretches. The original waterfront followed Willoughby to Front Street and around to South Franklin. The 1896 Lewis Building (now McDonald's at 130 Front Street) was one of the first claimed lots in town and was at the water's edge at high tide.

Several historic buildings cluster on or near Franklin Street.

KID STUFF

■ The Alaska State Museum hands out a free Kids' Guide to maps and Native culture exhibits. The guide's word games, riddles, and puzzles help explain the cultures of Northwest Coast Indians, Eskimos, and Aleuts. Don't miss the eagle tree diorama; ascend a spiral ramp to see it from all sides. At the top of the ramp, visit the children's gallery for a little dress-up or board a partial, one-third-scale model of Capt. Vancouver's ship *Discovery*.

■ Rev up your sweet tooth by watching chocolates dipped by hand and fudge tempered on marble slabs at the Alaskan Fudge Company (195 South Franklin Street; 907-586-1478).

■ Try your luck from the public fishing dock next to the Macaulay Hatchery (2697 Channel Drive, 3 miles from downtown). Remember, small fish can put up a big fight, so wear a life jacket.

To tour this area, begin at the **Governor's House** (716 Calhoun Street), an uphill walk from downtown. The white clapboard house (1912) has been termed "a liberal interpretation of New England colonial" architecture. It's not open to visitors except on rare occasions, such as an afternoon in December when thousands of cookies baked by the Governor's chef are gobbled by locals.

Flanking the front door of the Governor's House is a yellow-cedar totem carved by Charlie Tagook and William Brown of Klukwan and Saxman in 1939–40. Although known as the **Mosquito Legend pole**, this pole incorporates symbols of several Raven legends. The top two figures are Raven and Grandfather Raven, or Nass Shagi Yeil, "Chief at the head of Nass River." They recall the story of an earth in total darkness. Raven learned that Nass Shagi Yeil kept three cedar boxes in which he stored sources of light: the sun, moon, and stars. Raven journeyed to the head of Nass, transformed himself into a spruce needle, and was swallowed with a drink of water by Nass's daughter. The evergreen needle made her pregnant, and Raven was soon born as a child. The spoiled grandson cried for his grandfather's prized boxes as playthings, and liberated the sun, moon, and stars. This is one of the best-known Raven legends.

Another figure shows Haayee Shaanak'w or "Old Woman Underneath"—a spirit said to hold up the world on the foreleg of a beaver. One day, very hungry, Raven went to Old Woman Underneath and asked her to lower the ocean to make it easier for him to gather sea urchins to eat. At first she refused, but when Raven threatened her, she lowered the ocean's level. Since then, the world's oceans have risen and fallen twice a day.

The figure with the long beak is Mosquito. Above him is Guteel, a bogeyman figure. In prehistoric times, when hunters failed to return home Guteel was said to have eaten them. Eventually men decided to capture Guteel. They suceeded in luring him into a pit and setting him on fire, but as he approached his end, Guteel declared, "Even though you kill me, I will continue to bite you." His ashes flew into the air as innumerable mosquitoes.

Turn back toward downtown and look for a wooden overpass bearing a yellow sign, "13 ft. 7 in." Just before this overpass is a staircase heading down, down, down. (There's a bench on one landing.) Descend to Willoughby Avenue and you're at the site of the Aak'w Village. This was a summer fish camp until 1883, when Kowee and others moved here permanently to be nearer the cash economy. The beach line at that time followed where Willoughby is today.

Once on Willoughby Avenue, you'll be within easy reach of the **Alaska State Museum** (395 Whittier Street; 907-465-2901; www.museums.state.ak.us). If you'd like to bone up on local history and culture, follow the curve of Willoughby to your right, then turn left onto Whittier. You'll see the park-like setting of the museum one block ahead. The permanent exhibits focus on Alaska's Native peoples, Russian America, and the land's history after the American purchase. You'll see mementos such as bricks of tea used in early trade and gleaming Russian samovars.

If you're skipping the museum, simply follow Willoughby to its intersection with Gold Creek. Just over the bridge stands a **monument** to Harris and Juneau, marking the site of their original camp. If you head along the creek for about a block, it intersects with Egan Drive. From the bridges here, spawning salmon can be seen milling about in late August.

■ BRIEF EXCURSIONS

Get a lift from the **Mount Roberts Tramway** (907-463-3412). The tramway's base is near the cruise-ship docks; in six minutes you'll ride up 1,800 feet to an observatory complex which includes a restaurant, a bald eagle exhibit, a theater, and a nature center. Marmots sometimes dart about near the deck of the nature center. Check out the free film, *Seeing Daylight,* which gives a glimpse of Native culture from the Tlingit point of view. Native artists sometimes give demonstra-

MENDENHALL GLACIER

Seattle has its drive-up espresso stands, Las Vegas drive-up wedding chapels, and California . . . well, California may have a drive-up for just about anything, but none have Alaska's drive-up glaciers. Mendenhall Glacier is one of more than thirty glaciers that squeeze like toothpaste from the 1,500-square-mile Juneau Ice Field. . . . Each year 300,000 people visit this river of ice by bus or car and hundreds more on foot, bikes, roller skates, and cross-country skis in winter.

Yet with each passing year, Mendenhall becomes less approachable. Until 1750 the glacier was advancing, its face nearly two and a half miles closer to where Juneau was to be settled in the nineteenth century. Since then the glacier has retreated steadily—nearly three hundred feet in 2000 alone. In all the face has pulled back nearly a half mile from where it was when the visitor center was built in 1962. At some point in the not so distant future, the visitor center may have to be moved just to keep the glacier in view.

— Harry M. Walker, *Wacky & Wonderful Roadside Attractions of Alaska,* 2002

tions, or you might catch a tale from a Native storyteller. Fit hikers can walk down the Mount Roberts Trail in under an hour and a half, but keep in mind that it's steep and has lots of switchbacks—some with dramatic dropoffs.

Take in the **Taku Fisheries Ice House** (alley off South Franklin Street; no phone) on the sea side of the Twisted Fish Grill. Although from January through May Juneau appears to be a gabble of legislators and from May through September a gaggle of T-shirt vendors, it is a working fishing port. You can view the action first-hand at the Ice House. Fishing vessels anchor below the dock; their catches are unloaded at the top. The fish are either lifted in cargo nets, raised in totes (large plastic boxes), or whisked up through a tube resembling a giant dryer exhaust. Everything from halibut to gleaming silvers to bright orange rock fish is sorted here in season. Then saunter around the Grill to Taku's retail shop to sample smoked salmon.

Board a bus or taxi for the 12-mile ride to the **Mendenhall Glacier** (Glacier Spur Road; 907-789-0097). Mendenhall's drive-up accessibility makes it one of the world's most-visited glaciers, with over 300,000 sightseers a year. Along the easy switchback path to its visitors center (handicapped accessible, $3 fee), you can see grooves etched in the rock by moving ice. Inside the center, floor-to-ceiling windows open onto excellent views of Mendenhall Lake, which lies between the center and the glacier itself, and Photo Point Overlook. The lake is often dotted with small icebergs calved from the glacier's snout; the glacier itself is blue and white, streaked with brown. Peer through the telescopes on hand and you might spot grazing mountain goats. Photo Point Overlook, as the name suggests, is a favorite posing spot; locals often use Mendenhall as a backdrop for wedding photos. The center includes a handful of exhibits on glaciers, including a relief map of the ice field, a sample of rock flour (glacial silt), and displays defining such terms as crevasse, moraine, cirque, and plant succession. A short film on Mendenhall Glacier plays every 15 minutes in a comfortable theater. There are some kid-friendly displays too, such as a swatch of mountain-goat fleece.

The rocky promontory on which the visitors center was built in 1960 was once within arm's reach of the ice. In 1935 you could stand there and touch the face of the glacier—but since then the glacier has retreated more than a mile. Mendenhall has been receding for over 200 years. Between 1980 and 2000 its average loss was 90 feet a year. In 2004, however, it surprised the U.S. Forest Service by receding 600 feet—leading USFS to begin using the term "global warming." As the glacier retreats, it exposes bare rock that is gradually able to support vegetation. On your way to the visitors center, for instance, you'll pass cottonwoods, willows, and alder growing in shallow pockets of soil that have accumulated during the past century. Allow two hours for this excursion, not including the drive.

To stretch your legs, walk the easy 1½-mile Moraine Ecology Trail, or the half-mile Trail of Time. Or try the quarter-mile Photo Point Trail, which leads onto a peninsula of glacier-grooved and polished boulders, giving you good views of the glacier face and thundering Nugget Falls. A massive rock slide in 2005 made hiking out to the Falls, a round trip of about a mile, more difficult. As you move closer to the face, it's like stepping into a cold-storage facility. However, be careful not to disturb terns (small white birds) nesting on grass or sand on the flats around the lake.

Hundreds of miles of mining tunnels honeycomb Mount Roberts, but most are sealed off. One company, however, can get you in. Princess Tours (907-463-3900; www.princess.com) leads Juneau's only **underground mining tour** with A-J Mine/Gastineau Mill Enterprises. A van takes you to the ore-crushing plant and conveyer tunnel. Guides explain how stamps (rock crushers) work and how the ore traveled

(following pages) Ice meets ocean at the Tracy Arm Fjord, one of the world's most dramatic fjords.

from mine shaft to rock crusher. Walk into a mine shaft of what was once the world's largest producing gold mine and watch experienced miners demonstrate their noisy craft. (Hard hats and ear plugs are provided.) The tour takes about three hours.

For more mining memorabilia, visit the **Last Chance Mining Museum & Historical Park**, operated by the Gastineau Channel Historical Society (1001 Basin Road; 907-586-5338; $4). The museum occupies the restored compressor building (1912) of the Alaska-Juneau Mine, listed on the National Register of Historic Places. It's chockablock with machinery. The original compressor, which has a 750 horsepower motor, is not fired up because it would be deafeningly loud, but a Gade engine is occasionally started, going "chugga, chugga, *pooh!*" Be sure to check out the mock tunnel with tools and equipment. On the grounds are unrestored locomotives and passenger cars. Stroll from downtown to the end of Gold Street, then along scenic Basin Road for about three-quarters of a mile to the mine, reached via a footbridge. Basin Road provides excellent views across Gold Creek to Mount Juneau, where slide areas are evident and mountain goats can sometimes be seen grazing. Plan on at least two hours for the walk and visit.

Neophyte paddlers may head to the North Douglas boat ramp to take a **guided kayak trip** in the direction of Mendenhall Glacier. Alaska Travel Adventures offers this excursion (907-789-0052; www.bestofalaskatravel.com) in two-person kayaks, with escorts in motorized skiffs. The tour includes instruction, all gear, and a light snack. Of the 3½ hours involved, about 2 are spent paddling.

The Juneau Parks and Recreation Department sponsors **guided hikes** (907-586-0428; www.juneau.org/parkrec/hike/) on Wednesday and Saturday year-round. This is a good opportunity to meet locals and quiz them at length. For information about hiking trails, see the Trail Mix Web site, www.juneautrails.org.

Glacier Gardens Rainforest Adventure (7600 Glacier Highway, about 7 miles north of downtown; 907-790-3377) is a window into the Tongass National Forest that's a good choice primarily for travelers with mobility problems. This botanical garden shows what ingenuity and "sweat equity" can accomplish with a seemingly useless welter of mud. Owners Cindy and Steve Bowhay started their park in 1994 with seven acres of land ravaged by a landslide. Tree trunks and rocks were flung everywhere. The Bowhays channeled a meandering creek into ponds and repurposed uprooted trees. Steve imaginatively "planted" the fallen trees upside down to create "flower towers," using their flat root structures to grow petunias, fuchsias, and begonias in the sky.

The garden now encompasses 50 acres, including an eight-foot-wide golf-cart path to a boardwalk outlook. From this lookout point you'll have a panoramic view of the Mendenhall Wetlands, the shallow portions of Gastineau Channel, and the Lynn Canal. Golf-cart tours wind through a landscaped hillside area and up into uncultivated rain forest. Guides discuss the plants you'll see, and you might spot a river otter, an eagle, a falcon, or even a bear. Allow an hour to two hours for this tour. Visitors can stroll through the street-level gardens and greenhouses on their own, but an entrance fee is charged.

Head over to rocky Mayflower Island to see the **John Rishel Mineral Information Center** (907-364-1551), a lesser-known museum but a treasure trove if you're a fan of geodes and quartz crystals. On the first floor you'll find the Tom Pittman Geology and Mining Museum, stuffed with displays of hundreds of Alaska's minerals, from fool's gold to the real thing, as well as rock and fossil specimens. Historic photos and artifacts illustrate Juneau's gold-mining era. The center can easily be reached by public transportation or by car from downtown Juneau. (A short causeway connects Mayflower Island to Douglas Island.) Allow an hour for the trip.

Snapping the icebergs of Tracy Arm Fjord.

Treadwell Past and Present

The easy, two-mile **Treadwell Historic Trail** on Douglas Island leads through the remains of what was once a richly productive hard-rock gold-mining operation. Lulled by the trail's dappled light and birdsong, it's a mental stretch to visualize or "hear" the booming Treadwell complex that sprang up here at the turn of the 20th century. John Treadwell, the developer, created a far-reaching operation that ultimately included the Treadwell, Mexican, Ready Bullion, and 70-Foot mines, plus an entire company town. Seventy million dollars' worth of gold was mined here between 1882 and 1917.

To reach the trailhead from downtown Juneau, head across the Douglas Bridge, turn left, and walk three miles to the end of the road. The trail begins behind the picnic shelters at Sandy Beach, where a stamp (pulverizing mill) has been rescued from another location. During the mines' best years, 1900–1910, 880 such stamps thundered up and down 96 times a minute, pounding constantly 363 days a year. Miners operated in three eight-hour shifts and had only two holidays a year: the Fourth of July and Christmas.

Hundreds of miners were drawn here, and by the early 1900s a busy company town was in place. The boardinghouse fed 500 miners at a seating, while the Treadwell Club offered billiards and a 2,000-volume library. Groceries were delivered to homes by a St. Bernard pulling a wagon across the boardwalk. A large swimming pool, the Natatorium, was built in 1910, with showers, lockers, and dressing rooms as well as "a regular ladies day with a swimming instructor to teach them how to swim and dive."

In early 1909 there were 1,900 men on the payroll. A central shaft was sunk to 2,817 feet in 1916. But as tunnels bored deeper and drove beneath Gastineau Channel, the land became unstable. The ground surface began actively moving on February 1, 1917. The end came on April 21–22, when a stream the size of "the Yukon at White Horse rapids" began flowing into the Natatorium and the fire hall. Soon the main ore pit, the Glory Hole, collapsed. Luckily, not a single miner died in the collapse, but with the bells of the hoisting signals silenced, most of the employees soon moved on.

Walking the trail, you'll pass the Glory Hole, an assay office, and a massive water tank still tied to the Treadwell Ditch (a deep trough which collected water from several creeks). The area is honeycombed with shafts and pits, so stay on the trail. Along the way, bits of tram track and a huge steel water tank can be glimpsed in the underbrush. At the end of the trail, cyanide and arsenic (used in the ore extraction) have left their mark—no plants grow.

■ LONGER OUTINGS

One of the most popular day trips from Juneau is a boat trip to **Tracy Arm Fjord**. Thirty miles long, Tracy Arm is considered one of the world's most dramatic fjords—equal to any in Norway. Tucked away in a corner of the Tongass National Forest, 40 miles south of Juneau, the narrow fjord twists and turns between granite heights. Some of these cliffs climb 2,000 feet. During a cruise here you'll likely see waterfalls, seals resting on icebergs, and perhaps a bald eagle. At the head of the fjord you come face-to-face with the twin Sawyer Glaciers. Blue ice flows into the aquamarine ocean—the blue intensified if the day is overcast. When the snout of a Sawyer calves, you'll instantly grasp why the Tlingit name for one glacier was *Sumdum,* a rendering of the drum-roll noise of the calving. A cruise here takes about 9½ hours. Goldbelt Tours (800-820-2628; www.goldbelttours.com) is one of the companies to visit Tracy Arm. Its package includes lunch and a naturalist talk on the fjord. Adventure Bound (907-463-2509; www.adventureboundalaska.com) is another cruise company that offers visits to Tracy Arm with on-board naturalists.

If bear-watching tops your life list, make the effort to get out to **Pack Creek** on Admiralty Island. This island, on the far side of Douglas Island from Juneau, reputedly has the world's highest concentration of brown bears. At Pack Creek you can hike a mile to a viewing tower. If hiking through bear-infested territory makes your hair stand on end, you can instead watch from a spit where you can perch on a log, zero in with a telescope, and have a ranger at hand at all times. Peak season for observing brown bears noshing on salmon is July 5 to August 15. This is after the breeding season, and, since there is plenty of food, aggression between bears is limited. Pack Creek can be reached only by floatplane or boat. The Forest Service limits the daily number of visitors to 12, so you'll need to register in advance through the Admiralty Island National Monument office (907-586-8790). Flight services that access Pack Creek include Alaska Fly-N-Fish (907-790-2120), Alaska Seaplane Service (907-789-3331), and Wings of Alaska (907-789-9863). You'll need a day for this trip.

In September, visitors can sign up for a once-a-year event, Gastineau Channel Historical Society's **Lighthouse Cruise & Keeper's Lunch** (907-586-5338). This six-hour cruise takes you to the Sentinel Island, Eldred Rock, and Point Retreat lighthouses. Stop at Vanderbilt Reef for lunch, live music, and shipwreck/lighthouse history by members of the society.

Flightseeing over the icefield is a popular (and heavily marketed) activity in Juneau. For more information, *see* Flightseeing in the Practical Information chapter.

S K A G W A Y

Compact, breezy Skagway beckons from a northern finger of the Inside Passage. This seaport sits on a deep-water fjord, Taiya Inlet, at the head of Lynn Canal—a lovely 90-mile journey from Juneau between banks that seem untouched by human hands. When Klondike stampeder and budding author Jack London came here in 1897, he traveled in a Tlingit freight canoe. Oddly enough, London didn't describe this trip in any of the dozens of stories based on his northern experiences; perhaps it was simply too peaceful.

Skagway began as a lone cabin nestled on the delta fan of the Skagway River. The delta spills from a canyon, embraced on three sides by steep wooded slopes. Until 1970 Skagway did not have a road connection to the outside world. It could be reached only by railroad, ferry, and small aircraft. Today a well-maintained road leads to Carcross and Whitehorse, Yukon Territory, where it connects with the Alaska-Canada or Al-Can Highway. Tourism is now the town's main industry. Visitors often come wanting to learn some regional history. Some take to "the longest museum in the world"—the Chilkoot Pass Trail—while others simply walk Broadway, picturing the town in its gold-rush heyday.

■ SKAGWAY THEN

The original Skagway pioneer was crusty, loquacious Captain William "Billy" Moore, a former riverboat pilot. He and a Tlingit companion, Skookum Jim, hiked over the 45-mile White Pass route early in 1887 and thought it would do well as a route to the interior. Moore consequently staked claim to 160 acres on the delta fan of the Skagway River, built a log cabin, and became the area's first white settler. In the fall of 1887 he and his son Ben began constructing a wharf.

The settlement might have remained inconsequential but for an 1896 gold strike near Dawson City in the Klondike. When dozens of successful miners disembarked at major West Coast ports toting fortunes in gold nuggets and dust in July 1897, Americans were wrestling with a major economic depression. The dream of easy riches drew tens of thousands north—most of them to the sister ports of Dyea and Skagway. The first stampeders arrived in Skagway in August 1897. A tent city

The White Pass & Yukon Route Railway steams through the mountains.

Skagway boomed along with the Klondike Gold Rush. Now its historic district is a tourism magnet.

FAQs:

Who was Captain Moore?

Captain William Moore was a tough man with the ability to predict settlement patterns. The former riverboat captain was rugged enough to secure the first contract to deliver mail in the Yukon in 1896—at age 74. He is sometimes called the "discoverer" of the White Pass Trail. (It had probably been used for centuries by Tlingit traders.) Moore's claim to fame is twofold. First, he believed that gold would be discovered in the Yukon Valley. Second, he guessed that the White Pass Trail would be important for access to the Yukon. He put his stamp on his theories by staking claim to 160 acres on Skagway Bay and becoming its first Caucasian settler in 1887, ten years before George Carmack's bonanza gold discovery became common knowledge.

What does "skookum" mean?

Skookum is a term in the Chinook trading language meaning "strong," "big," or "replete with rapids." The Chinook trad-

SKAGWAY

0   250   500 Feet

**Map labels:**

To Klondike Hwy. Carcross, Y.T. 67 mi. Whitehorse, Y.T.

To Gold Rush Cemetery

To Hanousek RV Park

10th Ave
9th Ave
8th Ave
7th Ave
6th Ave
5th Ave
4th Ave
3rd Ave
2nd Ave
1st Ave

Main St
State St
Broadway
Alaska St
Spring St

City Hall

Skagway Inn (1897)

Trail of '98 Museum

Post Office

Eagle Hall

William Moore Cabin (1887)

Airport Terminal

Historic District

Skagway Home Hostel

Arctic Brotherhood Hall, City Visitor Information & Public Restrooms

Dewey Lakes Trail

Shagway Brewing Co

White Pass & Yukon RR Depot

Soapy Smith's Parlor

National Park Service Visitor Center

To Dyea, Dyea Campground, Slide Cemetery & Trailhead for Chilkoot Trail, 9 mi.

Dyea Rd

Airstrips

Yakutania Point Trail

Skagway River

Pullen Pond

Pullen Creek RV Park

Ore Terminal

Broadway Cruise Ship Dock

Float Plane Dock, Chilkat Cruises and Tours & Haines-Skagway Fast Ferry

Cruise Ship Terminal

Cruise Ship Terminal

State Ferry Dock

ing language was a basic, 250-word vocabulary used by voyageurs, prospectors, and Hudson's Bay traders for common terms like "food" and "bear." It was created by simplifying Chinook Indian words and combining them with scraps of other Native American words as well as French and English terms. Adventurer–authors like John Muir and Jack London picked up bits of this language and used them in their prose for local flavor.

What is the origin of the name Skagway?

This place name derives from the Tlingit term meaning "place where the north wind blows" or "home of the north wind." In other words, hold onto your hat!

Klondike prospectors and their goat-drawn sled of supplies, ca. 1898.

quickly sprang up. During the two years of the Klondike Gold Rush, over 100,000 stampeders would be infected with "Klondicitis." Newcomers were called *cheechako* ("tenderfoot" or "greenhorn"). Experienced prospectors were dubbed "sourdoughs," because they often used sourdough starter as the yeast in bread and flapjacks.

Skagway quickly became a lawless boomtown where bunco artist Jefferson Randolph "Soapy" Smith and his gang of hoodlums and "sure thing" men fleeced unwary cheechakos as they arrived, and robbed successful sourdoughs returning from the Klondike. The sound of occasional gunfire mingled with the constant sound of hammers and the whine of Billy Moore's sawmill. More than 700 new frame structures rose above the original tents in the first four months of the rush. Every week at least two steamships arrived freighted with optimistic men and women planning to hike over the White Pass from Skagway or the Chilkoot Pass from Dyea. Both routes scaled the 6,000-foot coastal range that separates the Canadian interior from the American coast. Moore put the word out that White Pass was lower than the Chilkoot, and that since it was clear of boulders (unlike the Chilkoot), pack animals could take food and supplies all the way from tidewater to Lake Bennett. And then it was just 450 miles to Dawson and the gold fields.

A December 31, 1897, article in *The Skaguay News* by Annie Hall Strong encouraged women to join the stampede. Strong claimed she expected to find "mobs of evil-doers" but instead found "everything orderly and quiet . . . no evidence of violence or crime—nothing but kindness." There were 3,000 people in Skagway at this time, Strong wrote, and the insta-town had a church, a school, electric lights, and a telephone system.

On July 1, 1898, *The Skaguay News* proclaimed Skagway "a marvelous city," predicting that the town was "entering the threshold of an era of prosperity unparalleled in the annals of Alaskan history." That prosperity was to come "in the shape of the Skaguay and Lake Bennett railroad—the first and only line . . . that anyone had ever, in the wildest flights of imagination, dreamed that Skaguay would have."

The newspaper's articles acted like press releases from a chamber of commerce on speed: "Here we can glorify and jollify with the full assurance that in no spot in the entire Union does the bright sun of prosperity beam more effulgently and with greater radiance than here in Skaguay, the metropolis of the northwest, the marvel of the last decade of the nineteenth century." Professional photographers including Eric A. Hegg, H. C. Barley, and Asahel Curtis captured dramatic moments along the wilderness trails, making the Klondike Gold Rush the most-photographed event of the day. Magazines and newspapers from around the world dispatched reporters for first-hand stories, stoking the stampede.

The reality was far from bright and wholesome. In the summer of 1898 some 15,000 people were living in tents, shacks, and crude rooming houses. Skagway had 61 saloons, an equal number of gambling dives, three breweries, and dance halls from which drifted tunes like "There'll Be a Hot Time In The Old Town Tonight." Specialty acts like knife throwers, acrobats, trained dogs, female performers, and magicians were imported to amuse miners—and separate them from their cash. Superintendent Samuel Steele of the Royal North West Mounted Police described it as "the roughest place in the world, little better than a hell on earth."

Steele was particularly infuriated by Soapy Smith. The con man was a skilled sleight-of-hand artist with a variant on the usual walnut shells and hidden pea game; he used bars of soap, hence the nickname. Gold-mad Skagway offered in spades the ingredients Soapy needed to work his swindles—desperate men with plenty of cash and a swift population turnover. Soapy operated out of a saloon staffed by a bartender in a white jacket. This "parlor" fronted for marked-card games, muggings, robberies, and murders all the way from the docks to the White

ON THE CHILKOOT TRAIL

After a wonderful night's sleep, a hearty breakfast of cornmeal mush, bacon, and cold-storage eggs, condensed milk, prunes, and a whole orange—the last in the camp—and settling our hotel bill (meals and bunk $1 apiece), with high hearts that glorious July morning we started to climb that 3,000 feet of steep, narrow, icy mountain trail. The Indians said there was a curse on all who attempted it in summer, as the hot sun melted the winter snow, and it came crashing down. . . . These avalanches had already taken toll of nearly 100 lives.

For the first hour we walked over the trail of the recent slide. In the melting snow I saw a bit of blue ribbon. Bending down, I tugged at it and pulled out a baby's bootee. Did it belong to some venturesome soul who had come to seek a fortune for wife and baby? Would those who were waiting for him wait in vain? . . .

I did not dare look round at the magnificent mountain scenery nor drink in the beauty of the tumbling torrents, for every minute the melting snow was making it more slippery under foot. . . .

As the day advanced the trail became steeper, the air warmer, and footholds without support impossible. I shed my sealskin jacket. I cursed my hot, high, buckram collar, my tight heavily boned corsets, my long corduroy skirt, my full bloomers which I had to hitch up with every step. We clung to stunted pines, spruce roots, jutting rocks. In some places the path was so narrow that, to move at all, we had to use our feet tandem fashion. Above, only the granite walls. Below, death leering at us. . . . In my agony I beg the men to leave me—to let me lie in my tracks, and stay for the night.

—Flo Whyard (ed.), *Martha Black: Her Story from the Dawson Gold Fields to the Halls of Parliament*, 2003

Pass. Soapy made nice with settled Skagway residents, but he also conducted profitable scam businesses, such as a telegraph to nowhere.

After Soapy Smith was shot dead in a duel with town surveyor Frank Reid in July 1898, life in Skagway became safer and even rather civilized. Newspaper ads turned from miners' supplies and portable Yukon stoves to bathtubs and "fine toilet seats." In 1900 the newly constructed White Pass & Yukon Railway to Lake Bennett promoted itself as the "Scenic Route of the World," and the Pacific Coast

The Arctic Brotherhood Hall, where members gathered for "fun, fight, or footrace."

Steamship Company assigned three ships to the summer Alaskan tourism trade. With its population at 15,000, Skagway was at this time the largest city in Alaska.

When the rush to the Klondike dwindled and stampeders headed instead to destinations such as Nome and Fairbanks, the population of Skagway quickly declined. By 1910 there were only a few hundred residents. Gold production in the Yukon fell off through the 1930s, and gold mines in Alaska were shut down during World War II. But military storage at Skagway helped to keep the town going through the war.

■ SKAGWAY NOW *map page 111*

Although Dyea has become a ghost town, Skagway thrives, a beehive of tourist activity—at least for half the year. In fact, many Skagway sites remain much the same as they were in the hectic days of 1897–98, right down to the false fronts that pretend one-story buildings rise to two stories, the wooden sidewalks, and the gleaming dome of the Golden North Hotel (1898). Billy Moore's cabin is still

(following pages) Skagway tourists then (the turn of the 20th century) and now.

HAPPY HOOLIGAN'S ARRIVING AT SKAGWAY MAY 8 1905

40 Vaudville & dance house
enroute to interior of yuk
Simons & Blakes outf.
1905.

TAILORING.
CLEANING & REPAIRING.
H. BOAS.

VIEWS: WHITE PASS-DAWSON.
Jegg PHOTOGRAPHER

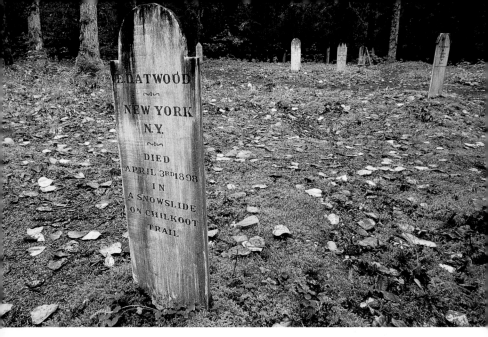

Victims of circumstance in Dyea's Slide Cemetery.

here, as is Jeff Smith's Parlor, although both have been moved to new locations. The original, one-story Brackett's Trading Post (1897) was moved to Broadway and restored in the 1980s by the National Park Service. The neat network of streets remains as it was laid out by surveyor Frank Reid—the man who shot Soapy Smith in a confrontation on one of the town's wharfs. (Reid died too, several days later, from the wounds he received.)

An example of the local commitment to the town's history is the Klondike Gold Rush National Historic Park. This park was established in 1976 after decades of local lobbying. It's an unusual setup, split between Washington and Alaska. The northern segment includes Skagway's historic structures, the deserted Dyea town-site, the White Pass Trail to the boundary with Canada, and the first 17 miles of the Chilkoot Trail. Another special link to the past is the White Pass & Yukon Railway. After a hiatus in the 1980s it relaunched its passenger service from Skagway to Lake Bennett and is now a top visitor attraction.

Skagway is renowned for its gardens. Long hours of "midnight sun" and the dew that accumulates during the evening stimulate speedy growth, especially of fragrant sweet peas, enormous dahlias, and tart, rosy rhubarb. Fair weather is likely here, as precipitation in Skagway averages only 26 inches a year—but keep a scarf handy for the wind.

Kid Stuff

■ Count the pieces of driftwood on the front of the Arctic Brotherhood Hall. During the winter of 2004/05 the city repaired, restored, and replaced 8,000 of the 20,000 chunks of driftwood on this structure—one of the most-photographed in town.

■ Combine trains and flowers at **Jewell Gardens** (Klondike Highway; 907-983-2111). Just over the bridge crossing the Skagway River, the showy garden includes flowers, organic vegetables, and a model railroad. The G-scale railroad winds through a model town that resembles Skagway in Soapy's day, complete with a tent city. While you watch the trains puff-puff into tunnels, you can sit down with a proper cup of English tea, a wedge of smoked salmon quiche, or a nasturtium sandwich with herbed cream cheese.

This tight-knit community has only about 800 year-round residents, but it's expected to draw about a million visitors by 2007. It may sound theme park–ish, and there's no denying the summer crowds, but the town's careful restoration is impressive. If you're looking to bypass the high-season throngs, try for the "shoulder season" in early May or late September. But keep in mind that the weather may not be as cooperative and that some of the souvenir shops close as the owners head south for the winter.

■ WALKING TOUR

The big draw is the **Klondike Gold Rush National Historic Park** (907-983-2921; www.nps.gov/klgo/), where you can walk in the footsteps of Captain Moore, Soapy Smith, and Jack London. The park is a joint effort of the United States and Canada.

The best place to walk is the downtown Skagway historic district section of this park. Take a self-guided tour of the 15 restored buildings by scanning the map available at the White Pass & Yukon Railroad Depot at Second Avenue and Broadway. In summer, rangers give 45-minute tours daily, but it's also a pleasure to just follow your nose. The historic building at Broadway and Seventh, now the Skagway Inn Bed & Breakfast, was established as a brothel in 1897. You'll find the Ben Moore House at Fifth Avenue and Spring Street. The park also includes a library and a display of artifacts such as a typical ton of goods loaded on a dog sled. Be sure to pause for the 30-minute film, *Days of Adventure, Dreams of Gold,* for an overview of life here during the gold rush.

The visitor information center is in the **Arctic Brotherhood Hall** (245 Broadway, near Second Avenue; 907-983-2854; www.skagway.com). You can't miss the building, as it's studded with pieces of driftwood. Built in 1899, this hall was headquarters for a secret fraternal organization whose members gathered for "fun, fight, or footrace."

To learn more about the town's history, hit the **Skagway Museum & Archive** (Seventh and Spring streets; 907-983-2420; www.skagwaymuseum.org). (This was formerly known as the Trail of '98 Museum, and is sometimes referred to as the "City Museum.") Exhibits and photographs cover all the highlights, like Moore's first crude wharf and sawmill, the tumult of the gold rush, the life and death of "Soapy" Smith, the railroad, and World War II. Native objects include a Tlingit canoe from Klukwan, carved halibut hooks, a bentwood box, and a Chilkat blanket.

For a scrimshawed version of Alaska's past, drop by the **Corrington Museum of Alaskan History** (Broadway and Fifth Avenue; 907-983-2637). It may share a space with a gift shop, but the collection is definitely worth a visit. Etched walrus tusks and ivory models commemorate dozens of events.

Plan on about three hours for this walk; a visit to the Skagway Museum will take another hour.

■ BRIEF EXCURSIONS

Attend a performance of the ***Days of '98*** show (Eagles Hall, Broadway and Sixth; 907-983-2545; www.alaskan.com/daysof98), a raucous musical melodrama based on Skagway's early history. Dramatis personae include Soapy, Molly Fewclothes, and Squirrel Tooth Alice. In other words, this is a bawdy show for adults. It goes on at 8 P.M. daily in summer, preceded by an hour of gambling demos.

The **Gold Rush Cemetery** is two miles from downtown. It's a walk on level ground, straight up State Street from the waterfront. Most of the graves in this quiet, wooded setting date from 1898 to 1904, and included are the markers for Soapy Smith and Frank Reid. Some of Soapy's critics didn't want him buried here, but the local reverend—to whose church he had made a sizeable donation— insisted he be in consecrated ground. **Flightseeing tours** via helicopter are available,

Bawdy performers at the Red Onion Saloon.

with spectacular views of glaciers and crevasses or a visit to Lake Bennett. Routes include tours of the Ferebee, Chilkat, or Meade glaciers—or dogsledding on the Denver Glacier. Allow about two hours for this outing. Among the major local operators are Skagway Air (907-983-2218; www.skagwayair.com) and TEMSCO Helicopters Inc. (907-983-2900 or 877-789-9501; www.temscoair.com).

Dyea was originally a Tlingit settlement guarding the trailhead for the Chilkoot, a prized trade route. The overgrown **Dyea Town Site** is nine miles northwest of Skagway. Rangers offer 1½-hour walking tours of this ghost town from mid-May through September, but don't provide transportation to the site. (If you don't have a car, try a cab, though these can be hard to find. Or you could rent a bike and ride, if you don't mind the bumpy gravel.) Register for the tour at the Historic Park. There's not much to see at Dyea other than wharf pilings, mysterious clearings among the evergreens, and the Slide Cemetery. A Palm Sunday avalanche in 1898 did in at least 60 people, and many who died in it are buried here. Legend has it that Soapy sent his henchmen to pick the corpses' pockets as they awaited burial.

Hubbard Glacier

The Hubbard Glacier is an icy tongue with its root on Mt. Logan in Yukon Territory. The vast Hubbard ice field originates near 15,300-foot Mt. Hubbard and flows 76 miles to lick the sea at Yakutat and Disenchantment bays. Many people access the glacier by floatplane from Skagway, Haines, or Yakutat. With its 400-foot snout, Hubbard Glacier is also a prime pausing point for cruise ships—especially for cruises with glacier themes. Hubbard calves great numbers of icebergs, making it difficult to get close. (There are no roads to the glacier. Unless you are a seasoned mountaineer with ice experience, Hubbard is no shore excursion.)

Yakutat, a town on the Gulf of Alaska, 225 miles northwest of Juneau, has some draws of its own. The scenery's magnificent, and there's world-class sport fishing for cutthroat trout, Dolly Varden, and king, silver, and sockeye salmon. The "Tat" (the river's nickname) is famed for white water. And you can certainly get away from it all, as there are no roads to Yakutat and the Alaska Marine Highway ferry stops there only when it has vehicles to unload.

The 24-million-acre international wilderness that embraces Hubbard can only be described with superlatives. For example, the massive St. Elias and Fairweather ranges are the largest nonpolar glaciated mountain system in the world. The region supports a population of both grizzlies and rare, silver-blue "glacier" bears.

This glacier is famous for "surging"—moving forward quickly. Most glaciers slide an inch or two a day. However, in 1986, the Hubbard Glacier made headlines around the world by advancing to the mouth of Russell Fiord, damming it, and creating a huge lake that lasted five months. By September it was advancing 30 meters a day. This was an event without precedent in recent geologic history.

Seals, sea lions, and porpoises were trapped behind the dam, and efforts were mounted to relocate them. "Russell Lake" eventually reached a level almost 90 feet higher than the level of Disenchantment Bay. When the dam broke on October 8 it produced an enormous rush of fresh water—something like a tidal wave in reverse.

The glacier surged again in summer 2002, creating another dam in the space of a month—by coincidence, just about the time glaciologists convened in Yakutat for an international symposium on fast glacier flow. Nervous Yakutat residents continue to lobby the government to build a channel to make sure the glacier cannot form "Russell Lake" again. They fear this would change river courses, endanger important fisheries, and inundate the Yakutat Airport, the chief transportation link with the rest of Alaska. For more on the current state of the Hubbard, see the U.S. Geological Survey site (http://ak.water.usgs.gov).

■ LONGER OUTINGS

If you don't mind breathtaking heights, board the narrow-gauge **White Pass &
Yukon Route Railway** (800-343-7373; www.whitepassrailroad.com) for a three-
hour excursion to rocky, 2,900-foot White Pass. You ride in cars from the mid-
20th century; an interpreter rides in every car to discuss the scenic highlights, like
Bridal Veil Falls. In order to feel like a fly on a cliff face, sit on the left side leaving
Skagway and on the right when returning. Fog occasionally rolls in, but most of
the time the views are spectacular. The tour is available from May through
September; because it's so popular, reservations should be made well in advance.

Sign up for **a day hike with Packer Expeditions** (907-983-2544). Packer leads
guided hikes in the area, including day and multiday hikes. Its most popular excursion is a 5½-hour jaunt involving a helicopter flight over the Juneau Ice Field; a
four-mile hike to Laughton Glacier; and a WP & YR ride back to Skagway. Packer
provides all gear, water, and snacks. But beware of glacier glare; wear sunglasses.

Take a hike from the Dyea trailhead over the **Chilkoot Pass Trail** (www.nps.
gov/klgo/chilkoot.htm). The entire Chilkoot trail is 32 miles and peaks at 3,246
feet. It crosses from Alaska into Canada, with fascinating variations in habitat
along the route. It's also a mile-wide "museum," as you'll see boot soles, horse
bones, enamelware coffee pots, collapsible canvas boats—all things that over-
burdened stampeders discarded on their way to Dawson City. You can photograph
these, but cannot disturb them. It's a challenging hike; you'll need to negotiate
snaking roots, slippery rocks, and mud. The "Golden Stairs" section has boulders
the size of railroad cars and smaller rocks that shift unnervingly underfoot. The
arduous trek takes most fit folk three to five days. Camping is restricted to locations where cook shacks are provided. While you won't have to haul a year's worth
of supplies over the pass, as 1897–98 stampeders did, you will need to shoulder a
tent, grub, and fuel. Bring rain gear, plus cords and a storage sack to hang your
food out of reach on bear poles. Before hiking in, check with the Historic Park for
the latest information on trail conditions and to get instructions for Canadian customs, which maintains an office at the top of the pass. It's difficult to get anyone in
Skagway on the phone during peak hours, so make your inquires well in advance.

H   A   I   N   E   S

Haines is set on Portage Cove, a gentle curve in the shoreline of Lynn Canal. Like Skagway, Haines is a compact spot, with a downtown half a dozen blocks wide and half a dozen blocks deep, although there are some "suburbs" slowly rising in the direction of Chilkoot Lake and Battery Point Trail. You won't find highrises— except for the natural backdrop, the jagged, 6,500-foot Cathedral Peaks. These make a stunning "stage set" for the dress parade of white clapboard officers' residences at Fort William H. Seward.

Some tourists dash through on their way to what they consider "bigger fish" like Kluane National Park. But Haines is worth an overnight stay. For one thing, Haines is one of the drier spots on the Inside Passage, averaging 2 inches of precipitation per month during the summer. Around the summer solstice you can expect about 20 hours of daylight during which to explore.

Haines is one of the few Inside Passage cities connected to other road systems. The Haines Highway follows the general route of a packhorse trail to the Klondike used by prospectors in the late 1880s. This 44-mile highway connects Haines with Haines Junction in Canada's Yukon Territory. When the threat of invasion from Japan rose in World War II, the road was improved for military access for the U.S. Army. If you drive the route now—a trip of about an hour—you will see coastal rain forest gradually give way to alpine tundra.

■ HAINES THEN

The first humans to settle in the Chilkat Valley were Tlingits. They seem to have established a site at Klukwan, 22 miles up the Chilkat River. Klukwan was reputedly the first village, but a second large settlement was established near Chilkoot Lake, five miles north of the modern ferry dock. Before 1881 there was nothing permanent at the site of modern Haines—just a summer fish camp with temporary shelters and fish-drying shacks slightly to the northwest. At this fish camp, called Dei Shu, or "end of the trail," Chilkat and Chilkoot Indians traded first with Russian and then with American ships.

A rare road along the Inside Passage: the Haines Highway.

HAINES

0   ¼   ½ Miles

0   ¼   ½   ¾ Kilometers

**Map labels:**

Allen Rd

To
State Ferry Terminal 5 mi.
Chilkoot River, 8.7 mi.
Chilkoot Lake State Park, 11 mi.

View St

Union Ave

Dalton Ave

6th Ave

5th Ave

4th Ave

3rd Ave

2nd Ave

Front St

Main St

State Park
Information Center

Tsirku Canning
Co. Museum

Haines Hwy

To
Haines Junction, 159 mi.
Klukwan, 22 mi.
Eagle Council Grounds 19 mi.
Airport, 4 mi. &
Canadian Border, 42 mi.

Alaska Backcountry
Outfitters

Library

Alaska Nature Tours

City Hall

American Bald Eagle Foundation

Southeast
Alaska State
Fairgrounds
(old Dalton
City)

Visitor
Center

Health Center

Front St

Sheldon Museum and
Cultural Center

Portage Cove

Lookout
Park

Tlingit
Park

Cox

Post
Office

Bay

Mud

Ft. Seward Rd

Totem St

Portage St

Beach

Cruise Ship Terminal

Port Chilkoot Dock

Chilkat Cruises
Dock

Fort Wm. H. Seward
(Port Chilkoot)

Chilkat Tribal
House

Theater Rd

Rd

N
W   E
S

FAA Rd

Tower Rd

Battle Rd

Chilkat Center

Alaska Indian Arts

To
Portage Cove Campground, .75 mi.
Battery Point Trailhead, 1.5 mi.

FAQs:

What's the connection between Haines and Darth Vader?

Actor James Earl Jones, who was the voice of Darth Vader, commissioned a totem from Alaska Indian Arts, an organization based in Haines. The 22-foot pole, completed in 2001, has a four winds design in homage to his Choctaw heritage.

Where are the bald eagles?

The local quipster's reply is "look up." Truth is, during the summer eagles fade away to a variety of feeding spots. It's in autumn that they concentrate around Haines in large numbers. The Alaska Chilkat Bald Eagle Preserve is considered one of Alaska's top ten visitor destinations.

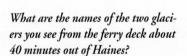

Annual salmon runs bring bald eagles—and visitors—in droves.

What are the names of the two glaciers you see from the ferry deck about 40 minutes out of Haines?
The first one spotted along the shores of the fjord called Lynn Canal is the Davidson Glacier. The Rainbow Glacier comes next. Both icy tongues flow out of one of the ice fields of Glacier Bay National Park.

In addition to the fish runs, bald eagles, which flock to the valley in fall and winter, may have been part of the area's attraction for the Chilkoot and Chilkat tribes. Eagles are an important symbol in Tlingit culture. The Tlingits established important trade routes into the interior. These were called "grease trails" because the most valuable item carried over them was eulachon or hooligan oil, rendered from small fish that run each May. (Hooligan are so oily that they're nicknamed "candle fish," because you can insert a wick into a dried fish and use it like a candle.) The grease, stored in hollow kelp or bentwood boxes, was exchanged for copper, obsidian, and furs.

In 1879 naturalist John Muir and his friend Presbyterian missionary S. Hall Young scouted the area with the help of Tlingit guides. Two years later, Young assigned two Presbyterians to found a mission, which was named for a Presbyterian fundraiser, Francina Haines. Muir was stunned by the sheer bulk of spawning salmon he saw here: "Their numbers are beyond conception. Often-times there seem to be more fish than water. . . . Surely in no part of the world may one's daily bread be more easily obtained." Canneries naturally followed in 1882, with up to nine operating at the peak of the industry.

A gold rush–era trading post, ca.1895–1897.

Anticipating gold rushes in the interior, American entrepreneur Jack Dalton "mined the miners" by turning a grease trail into the Yukon into a 305-mile toll road. He began construction on the road in 1891; eventually the trail linked Pyramid Harbor (west of Haines) with Fort Selkirk on the Yukon River. Dalton established trading posts along his trail, and by 1899 the U.S. government had granted him permission to charge fees. However, by 1900 competing routes established by miners reluctant to line Dalton's pockets put Dalton essentially out of business.

Fort William H. Seward—named after the U. S. secretary of state who championed the Alaska Purchase—stands on a knoll half a mile south of downtown Haines. The fort was proposed in 1902 because of an ongoing border dispute between the United States and Canada. When it was completed in 1904, it became the first permanent army post in Alaska and was considered "foreign-duty." (It was renamed Chilkoot Barracks in 1923, then re-renamed Fort Seward when it became a National Historic Landmark in 1978.) If you're arriving by water, you'll spot its distinctive white Victorian-style officers' quarters as you approach town.

Haines was incorporated in 1910. In the early 1920s Haines, like many small, struggling frontier towns, competed for settlers, printing leaflets trumpeting its attractions. In 1924 Haines tooted its own horn with a large sign across its main street: "Haines, Alaska, is the natural gateway to Porcupine, Rainy Hollow, White Run and Tanana valley, have Vast Resources of gold, silver, copper, lead, iron, and coal. Large areas of farming, grazing, and timber lands. Best climate of any city or town on the coast of Alaska." That year the population was about 300. Tlingits were employed at a cannery seven miles out of town, and there was a sawmill half a mile north. Like most communities along the Inside Passage, Haines was accessible only by sea and air until a flurry of war-related construction linked it to the rest of the world by road in 1943.

After World War II the decommissioned fort was sold to a group of veterans. Mimi and Ted Gregg and Carl Heinmiller were among those offered homesteads, and, captivated by Haines, they made a gutsy decision. They recognized that the Tlingit heritage was dying out and resolved to establish training programs to preserve Tlingit arts, including woodcarving, sculpture, block printing, textile design, lapidary work, and Native dance. Their programs were a success and continue to this day.

THE SCALPEL AND THE AX

There is a huge scientific debate ranging in the Tongass over what kinds of wind-storms may have begotten the forest we see today. In some places, huge gales occasionally sweep the forested mountain slopes, leaving twenty-acre piles of felled trees. A study of one island on the Tongass suggested that these intense storms may have affected a sizable percentage of the area—providing a perfect excuse for those who favor massive clear-cuts to say their logging is simply an emulation of nature. But the forest tells a much more complex story. It is not a large patchwork like a nice orderly tapestry we might want to weave, but a mosaic, every piece a different shape, each overlapping some others, and all with a different story of disturbance. If only we could more easily adopt the view of one of these patriarchs, it would be so much easier to see what is important, what is the scalpel and what is the ax, where and how often each force plays a role, and to what ultimate effect.

—Paul Alaback, "The Tongass Rain Forest—An Elusive Sense of Place and Time,"
in: *The Book of the Tongass*, 1999

■ HAINES NOW *map page 126*

You might well breathe a sigh of relief when you reach Haines. Fewer cruise ships dock here than in Juneau or Skagway, so the mood is serene. As Lee Heinmiller (Carl's son) puts it, "It's an actual real community—not Knott's Berry Farm of the North." Several stately homes along Officers' Row have been recycled as Victorian bed-and-breakfasts, where you can sit on the porch and smell the lilacs or sweet william. Local writer Heather Lende calls Haines "a small town where everybody waves and you don't have to lock your doors." The population hovers at about 1,800.

Haines is to bald eagles what Pack Creek is to brown bears. The stately birds flock to the Chilkat Valley because the warm open water of its rivers and its spawning salmon make for a comfortable food source well into cold weather. As the salmon finish spawning in fall, they begin to die off—the perfect eagle meal. Several hundred eagles live here year-round, but an additional 3,000 arrive each November, resulting in the world's largest gathering of eagles. The Alaska Bald Eagle Festival celebrates this event for a week every November. The best place to

The jagged Cathedral Peaks set off the tidy buildings of historic Fort Seward.

watch the eagles is at the Alaska Chilkat Bald Eagle Preserve (*see* Brief Excursions, below). There's also an eagle museum downtown if you'd like to bone up on the birds.

As in the days of John Muir, fishing is a major attraction. Fishing sites include Chilkat State Park (7 miles south of Haines on Mud Bay Road), Chilkoot Lake State Recreation Site (12 miles north of Haines, off Lutak Road), and Mosquito Lake State Recreation Site (about 30 miles north of Haines along the Haines Highway). All three sites have fire rings, toilets, potable water, picnic tables, and a boat launch.

Haines is a base from which to travel to Glacier Bay, Skagway, or the Yukon. Alaska Marine Highway ferries stop here on their trips north from Bellingham, Washington. Skagway is just 35 minutes away by water taxi (catamaran) from mid-May to mid-September. And there is a daily 2½-hour ferry service from Juneau (Chilkat Cruises & Tours; 888-766-2103).

■ WALKING TOUR

If you start your walk from the Port Chilkoot Dock, walk along the beach or turn right on Beach Road. You'll pass the Welcome Totems Park, where poles depict bears, eagles, and salmon. Turn left on Main Street, go two blocks, and then make another left on Second Avenue to check in at the **Haines Convention & Visitor Bureau** (122 Second Avenue South; 800-458-3579). If you plan to see Fort Seward, pick up the free pamphlet *A History and Walking Tour of Fort William H. Seward.* From here, turn right on Second Avenue and return to Main Street. Turn right again and look for the **Hammer Museum** (108 Main Street; 907-766-2374), where hundreds of antique and modern hammers speak to one man's esoteric fascination. A block away is the **Sheldon Museum & Cultural Center** (11 Main Street; 907-766-2366). The Sheldon's displays focus on Tlingit art and culture typical of the area, the Haines Mission, and pioneer history. The museum's collection is based on objects collected by pioneers Steve and Elisabeth Sheldon, who married here in 1913. As you leave the Sheldon, turn left onto Main Street and head to the **Tsirku Canning Company Museum** (Fifth and Main streets; 907-766-FISH). Here you can watch a restored canning line in action; all the equipment dates from the 1920s.

This would be a good time to break for lunch. (There are several casual lunch spots downtown.) Afterwards, if you're still raring to go, head left down Main Street toward Portage Cove, then turn right on Front Street. Take a detour into the small boat harbor to snap some photos, if you wish, or continue along Front (which parallels the shoreline) until you reach Portage Street. Turn right on Portage Street, then curve left on Second Street, and **Alaska Indian Arts** will be on your left (24 Fort Seward Drive; 907-766-2160; www.alaskaindianarts.com). AIA has been an important force in the revival and perpetuation of Northwest Coast art and performance since 1947. The organization's home base has a cultural history display, plus totem carving, silverwork, and printmaking. You can watch totem carvers, Chilkat blanket weavers, and silversmiths at work. Prints, weavings, and silver jewelry can be purchased, and totems can be commissioned.

Renamed in 1972 and declared a national historic site, **Fort Seward** celebrated its 100th anniversary from 2002 to 2004. You can walk around the grounds or call naturalist/photographer Joe Ordonez for a custom tour (907-766-3576; joeorga@hotmail.com). You can even stay here overnight at the Hotel Halsingland, on the fort's grounds (*see* the Practical Information chapter). The hotel has the town's only full-service restaurant.

This walk would take roughly five hours, including a lunch break.

Haines is set on gentle Portage Cove.

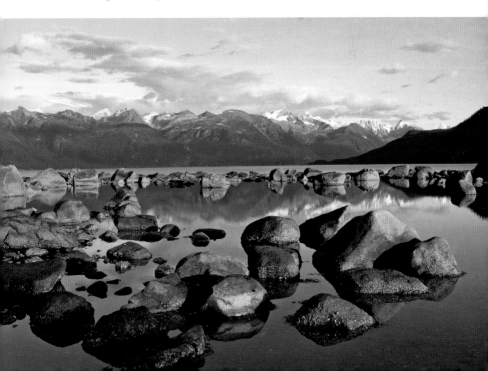

LET THE MASK BUYER BEWARE

Chilkat dancer, ca. 1955.

From the first days of trade between explorers and Northwest Coast peoples, art played a role. Indians at Nootka Sound, in British Columbia, left masks on board visiting ships—apparently as gifts. One captain described this occurrence: "Natives would sometimes bring strange carved heads and place them at a conspicuous part of the ship and desire us to let them remain there, and for this they would receive no return." Both Captain James Cook (1778) and Captain George Vancouver (1792) carried cedar masks, daggers, rattles, basketry, and intricately carved fishhooks back to England. The masks were realistic, dramatic, and colorfully painted. Museums were delighted to have them.

Masks are still avidly collected for their aesthetic appeal. However, buyers should beware of copies created in production workshops in Bali and other countries. Balinese carvers use reference books to research traditional Tlingit, Eskimo, Kwakiutl, and Haida designs. In other words, "bargains" are sometimes *not* good deals but imported copies by non-Natives. An artist's signature is no guarantee, because workshops make a practice of purchasing the rights to Native names or coining Native-sounding names.

Take precautions: Ask for a certificate of authenticity. Buy directly from carvers working on-site or from Native artists with their own galleries. Those who know Pacific Northwest or Inuit art well may recognize a copy if it looks out of proportion or has non-traditional paint colors. Black, red, brown, yellow, blue-green, and white paint are long-established colors, but pink, blue, or orange paint aren't in the traditional palette.

If a shop owner refers to a "local artist," he may mean a Canadian. If shop owners insist on playing 20 questions about the identity of an artist, thank them—and move on.

Another tip: Inspect each mask carefully. If carved from green wood, it may have hairline cracks in several places.

KID STUFF

■ Fans of loud noises should take in the unique **Hammer Museum** (108 Main Street, uphill from the harbor). About 1,200 hammers are on display—from mighty implements for forging swords to tiny tack hammers for upholsterers. You can lift a few, including a two-handled hammer. Kids under age 13 get in free.

■ Strap on your imaginary Colt 45 and explore **Dalton City**, the set for the movie *White Fang*, at the Southeast Alaska State Fairgrounds, off the Haines Highway about 1/3 mile from downtown. It's like walking a frontier street of the 1890s, though the buildings are reproductions. If you're here in August, the state fair will be in full swing (*see* Brief Excursions, below).

■ For close encounters with indigenous wildlife such as lynx, wolves, woodland caribou, and wolverines, visit **Kroschel Park** (Mile 1.5, Mosquito Lake Road, 30 miles north of Haines; 907-767-5464). This 40-acre sanctuary is the baby of Steve Kroschel, and his stock is mostly orphaned, hand-raised young 'uns. Species that need extra room, such as wolves, are kept in large compounds. There are usually some animals that can be touched, such as the Arctic fox.

■ BRIEF EXCURSIONS

The **Alaska Chilkat Bald Eagle Preserve** (Haines Highway; 907-766-2292; www.dnr.state.ak.us/parks/units/eagleprv.htm), created in 1982, spreads its protective wings over 48,000 acres bordering the Chilkat, Klehini, and Tsirku rivers. Logging and mining are illegal here, but the harvesting of naturally replaced resources such as berries and fish is permitted. The best observation areas are accessed from pullouts along the Haines Highway, between 19 and 26 miles from town. There is nothing like being on the riverbank in December as mists curl upward and thousands of screaming eagles fight over salmon carcasses. (Eagles have several calls, including a high fluting cry that definitely gets your attention.) If you're here in spring, especially April, you'll have a good chance of seeing the spectacular courtship behavior, when the birds lock talons in flight and cartwheel earthward. To learn more about eagles before you go, visit the **American Bald Eagle Foundation** (113 Haines Highway; 907-776-3094; www.baldeaglefest. org). This education center displays a diorama of the Chilkat preserve, taxidermied specimens, and a video.

EAGLES AND RAVENS

Along the Inside Passage, eagles and ravens are not simply regal, high-soaring creatures. They're also symbols of the two main divisions of Tlingit society—as meaning-
ful as donkey and elephant to Democrats and Republicans. The Tlingit word for
"eagle" is *ch'aak*—which sounds something like a cry the eagle makes. The Tlingit
word for "raven" is *yeil*. A hundred myths lie behind the raven's jet stare.

Mature eagles with their white heads and tail feathers are the largest, most visible
of the 300 bird species that live here. Their wingspans stretch between six and eight
feet; the females are slightly larger than the males. About half of all bald eagles in the
world live in Alaska. About one quarter of those, or 10,000 breeding pairs, construct
their large platform nests along the Inside Passage. Amended year after year, a nest
can weigh 2,000 pounds. Although carefully hidden, most nests are within 200 yards
of water, so that the parents can be close to fishing grounds for the 70 to 90 busy
days they are feeding their chicks.

How can you tell a raven from a crow? Although both are sleek and black, the
raven is larger and has a more massive bill. While crows flock in groups of up to 50
birds, ravens tend to be solitary or to fly in pairs. The Tlingit considered ravens to be
very intelligent, clever, and even tricky—basing more than 100 myths on their
antics. Bold and curious, a raven has a confident stride in the city and is not easily
spooked. Ravens will eat almost anything, from sea urchins to roadkill porcupines.
They have 17 distinct calls—expressing messages such as "humans approaching" and
"lots of food over here."

Although they compete for some of the same foods, ravens and eagles may mingle
to "kettle." This is flying in a languid spiral, taking advantage of mountain updrafts.

These two raptors have inspired Tlingit art; for example, a certain type of Chilkat
blanket with black tassels is known as the "raven's tail." Both ravens and eagles often
appear as masks or on totem poles. A raven is carved with a straight beak, while an
eagle's beak is curved or hooked. Look for these birds in the designs beaded on ceremonial vests and headbands too.

(left, at top) Bald eagles flock to their feeding grounds.
(left, at bottom) And photographers follow them.

Sample the award-winning onion wine, Zwiebel, produced by **Great Land Wines** (25 Small Tracts Rd., about a mile from Port Chilkoot Dock; 907-766-2698; www.greatlandwines.com). The vintners try to duplicate wines from the Gold Rush era, including brews from rhubarb, dandelions, rose hips, and fireweed. The tasting room is, as the founder says, "beaucoup small," just big enough for four people at a time.

Hike to the summit of 1,760-foot **Mount Riley** for superb views of Lynn Canal, Taiya Inlet, and the Chilkat River. Read the *Haines is for Hikers* brochure (available at the visitors center) before you head out. The short, steep route (2 miles) begins 3 miles southeast of Haines on Mud Bay Road. The long, less difficult route (4 miles) begins on FAA Road behind Fort Seward.

August visitors can head to the **Southeast Alaska State Fair** (Dalton City; www.seakfair.org). Events include a women's logging show, a Most Lovable Dog contest, and a songwriters' competition. Kids gravitate to the carousel, game booths, and a fire-eating clown.

Salmon fishing on the Chilkat River.

■ LONGER OUTINGS

Klukwan, "Mother Village," is one of the only inland settlements in Southeast Alaska, and it's a treasure trove of Tlingit art. In 1984 several residents attempted to sell priceless Gaanaxteidi clan artifacts from the Whale House. House posts from that dwelling are considered some of the best Northwest Coast art in existence. Wrangling over ownership of village art has continued until the present, making today's villagers nervous about visitors. Because they want to raise funds for their own museum, elders now allow limited access. Keet Gooshi Tours can take you there (five person minimum; 877-776-2168; info@keetgooshi.com). The tour includes a ride through the Alaska Chilkat Bald Eagle Preserve, a visit to a traditional tribal house, presentations about the Tlingit people, and a demonstration of the preparation of "Indian butter" (eulachon grease). At the village you'll see carvings, some 200 years old, and Chilkat blankets. The art at Klukwan is worth a pilgrimage. The trip takes four to five hours.

Hard bodies are drawn to Haines for its climbing and mountaineering opportunities. Get a taste of the action with a half-day **rock-climbing** lesson with Alaska Mountain Guides & Climbing School (907-766-3366; www.alaskamountainguides.com).

Take a guided float trip on a multi-day **river expedition** on the Tatshenshini, Alsek, or Kongakut river with Chilkat Guides (907-766-2491; www.raftalaska.com). If you're short on time, you could sign up for the four-hour float trip on the Chilkat River.

Cross the Canadian border to visit the Yukon's **Kluane National Park and Reserve** (www.parkscanada.gc.ca/kluane), three hours north of Haines via the Haines Highway. Its St. Elias mountains will have you goggling. Woodland caribou sometimes stand in the road, Dall sheep clamber about, and there are 150 bird species, including the golden eagle. Adventurous visitors are attracted by the white water for which the Alsek River is famous. You'll need your passport to cross the border into Canada; your vehicle may be inspected. Canadian Customs is at Pleasant Camp, Mile 40.8 (907-767-5540). If traveling between September 15 and June 1, be sure to check on weather conditions (Alaska State Troopers in Haines, 907-766-2552; or Royal Canadian Mounted Police in Haines Junction, 867-632-5555).

GLACIER BAY
NATIONAL PARK AND PRESERVE

Red rivulets on a drifting ice floe at Johns Hopkins Glacier reveal that a harbor seal has just given birth. Suddenly the mother seal barks hoarsely. Tall, menacing black fins circle the floating nursery. Orcas, "wolves of the sea," angle for a tender pup lunch.

At the terminus of the Grand Pacific Glacier, birds wait for ice to calve so that they can feed on the shrimp and krill churned up by the turbulence. Mountain goats clamber up steep rock faces. Sea otters float on their backs in the surrounding water, cracking open clams with rocks.

Such activities are as much a part of the world of Glacier Bay as the polished rock marked by gouges or grooves called "glacial footprints." Naturalist John Muir wrote of this ecosystem, " . . . out of all the cold darkness and glacial crushing and grinding comes this warm abounding beauty and life to teach us what we in our faithless ignorance and fear call destruction is creation finer and finer."

■ GLACIER BAY THEN

Glacier Bay was once home to the Huna Tlingit. They arrived in the bay 3,500 years ago, but the Little Ice Age drove them out. Legend has it that as it drove away the Tlingit, the ice surged "faster than a dog could run," called down by a grumpy girl in puberty seclusion. The Tlingit name for the bay is *Sit'ee ti geiyi*, or "Place where the ice used to be." It's not all legend. Several cycles of glaciation have occurred in this region. The Tlingit then settled at Hoonah, although their cultural memories of the bay's rich resources—delicious seabird eggs, for example—remain strong.

This magnificent, 3.28 million-acre maze of inlets, islands, and glaciers was solid ice a mere 200 years ago. In July 1794 the HMS *Discovery* under the command of Captain George Vancouver was forced to drop anchor in Cross Sound because of the floating bergs in the area. Vancouver sent two longboats to survey, and his men sighted a five-mile-long bay. The 60-mile bay we know today was then just an indentation plugged by a cork of ice 300 feet high and five miles wide.

A cruise ship negotiates the watery maze of Glacier Bay.

CANADA
UNITED STATES

Muir Glacier

Riggs Glacier

1972
1976
1960
1948

Rendu Glacier

Carroll Glacier

1966

1966
1892

1966

1929

Wachusett

1929

1907

Casement Glacier

Adams Inlet

Tarr Inlet

1892

1892

RUSSELL
ISLAND

1880

Rendu Inlet

Queen Inlet

1907

1892

1860

1907

Muir Inlet

Lamplugh Glacier

Reid Glacier

1907

1892

1907

1879

1892

1919

1860

Glacier Bay

Tidal Inlet

1857

1845

Beartrack River

Brady Ice Field

1966

DRAKE
ISLAND

Beartrack Cove

1892

WILLOUGHBY
ISLAND

Wood Lake

Brady Glacier

Abyss Lake

Dundas River

Berg Bay

BEARDSLEE ISLANDS

Visitor Center
Glacier Bay Lodge

Park
Headquarters

1794

Bartlett Cove

Airport

1794

Gustavus

1750-80

1951

Dixon Bay

Dundas Bay

North Passage

PLEASANT
ISLAND

Icy Strait

Graves Bay

Taylor Bay

LEMESURIER
ISLAND

South Passage

N
W   E
S

Cape Spencer

INIAN
ISLANDS

GLACIER BAY
NATIONAL PARK
AND PRESERVE

0   5   10 Miles

0   5   10   15 Kilometers

Historical extent of glaciation

The lucky few who gain access to Glacier Bay will find an extraordinarily well-preserved environment.

FAQs:

What is "bergy seltzer"?

Bergy seltzer is the fizzing noise made when air that has been under pressure escapes from bubbles in glacier ice. It's also called "ice sizzle." Often cruise ships net a chunk of ice to give that "snap, crackle, pop" to preprandial cocktails.

Why is some glacier ice blue?

The blue color of glaciers derives from the pressures exerted on the ice crystals during the formation process. As the ice crystals change shape, they absorb longer light wavelengths and reflect back only short wavelengths, the blue end of the visible light spectrum. Glaciers appear bluer on overcast days—and they're easier to photograph when it's cloudy too. Blue ice becomes white as it is exposed to oxygen.

THE GLACIER AS ARCHIVIST

A glacier is an archivist and historian. It saves everything, no matter how small or big, including pollen, dust, heavy metals, bugs, bones, and minerals. It registers every fluctuation of weather. A glacier is time incarnate, a moving image of time: when we lose a glacier—and we are losing most of them—we lose history, an eye into the past; we lose stories of how living beings evolved, how weather vacillated, why plants and animals died. The retreat and disappearance of glaciers—there are only 160,000 left—means we're burning libraries and damaging the planet, possibly beyond repair. Bit by bit, glacier by glacier, we're living the Fall.

—Gretel Ehrlich, *The Future of Ice: A Journey into Cold*, 2004

Researching theories about glaciers that he had coined in Yosemite, John Muir first saw the bay in 1879, describing it as an "icy wildness unspeakably pure and sublime." In a Tlingit dugout canoe Muir explored a bay 48 miles long. Since about 1750 the bay has grown into a glittering nest of ice, with 12 tidewater glaciers, 30 alpine glaciers, and at least a dozen unnamed glaciers flowing out of the St. Elias Mountains into the arms of the bay. The land was designated a National Monument in 1920, a National Park and Preserve in 1980, and a World Heritage Site in 1992.

■ GLACIER BAY NOW *map page 144*

The community of **Gustavus** (pop. 350), the gateway to the national park, sits on a glacial moraine deposited as ice receded. "Downtown Gustavus" is the proverbial whistle stop—except there's no train. Beartrack Mercantile is the sole grocery store. The community had no electricity until 1990, and composting toilets and outhouses were the general rule until recently. But it's not utterly spartan here; there are several luxury lodges and B&Bs. The airport is surprisingly large, considering the size of the community; it was built in the 1940s to fuel military aircraft, because the weather here is often clearer than it is in Juneau, 65 miles away as the eagle flies. The cluster of buildings is near the airport at the eastern edge of the moraine, while Park Service Headquarters, a campground, Glacier Bay Lodge, and the boat dock are at Bartlett Cove at the western edge of the moraine, nine miles from anything else.

It's virtually impossible not to get a good glacier shot.

Over 350,000 people visit Glacier Bay annually—although large cruise ships do not stop. The National Park Service preserves the extraordinary marine environment by limiting entrance, and only two large vessels are permitted a day. ("Large vessels" are motor vessels of 100 U.S. gross tons or more carrying paying passengers.) Whoever lines up the best visitor programs wins the bidding process for these entry slots. Cruise ships in the preserve are generally from the Princess or Holland America lines; they offer interpretive programs, take rangers on board, and organize children's programs. Smaller tour boats can also jockey for admission; Alaska Sightseeing/Cruise West generally nets those slots. Permits run from midnight to midnight, so no vessels stay overnight. If you want to become intimately acquainted with the bay, you can arrange for flightseeing, fly-out sport fishing in Icy Strait, or guided day and overnight kayak trips.

Visitors usually yearn to hear the impressive "boom" of calving, when ice chunks break off the glacier faces. Calving is unpredictable, but one thing you can be sure of during a cruise here is a lesson in the cycle of plant succession.

When glaciers melt away, they expose bare rock. Traveling up Glacier Bay, you'll virtually head back in time, seeing the succession from the mature forest of Bartlett

Steller sea lions basking on South Marble Island

Cove to the naked earth at Margerie Glacier. After ice retreats and exposes bare rock, plant recovery begins with a black crust of algae. Next come horsetails and fireweed. As soil accumulates, willows and alders take hold. At the culmination of the process, hemlock and spruce trees grow up to 200 feet tall.

Weather stirs the pot. Storms whirl in off the Pacific, and when it rains on the bay it's snowing on the Fairweather Range, with its dramatic peaks like Mt. Fairweather (15,300 feet) and Mt. Crillon (12,726 feet). This snow builds up, compacts, and in 150 to 200 years gains enough weight to flow down from the mountaintops as a glacier. The glaciers here are retreating, though, and the warmer temperatures and shrinking ice seem to be spurring tourism. Some estimates guess that this national park's glaciers could vanish by 2030.

If you're not coming by boat, Alaska Airlines operates a daily round trip from Juneau to Glacier Bay on summer afternoons. Air Excursions will fly you over from Juneau for $70 one way. For details, contact the Gustavus Visitor Association (907-697-2454; www.gustavusak.com) or Glacier Bay National Park Headquarters (907-697-2230; www.nps.gov/glba).

■ BRIEF EXCURSIONS

Hit one of the two **hiking trails** near Glacier Bay Lodge. One is a mile-long nature loop. The other is the Bartlett Cove Trail, three miles round-trip. The latter offers a gander at the only mature spruce forest in Gustavus, the result of 200 years of plant succession since the glacier retreated from this terminal moraine. Fallen trees show the force of winter gales. Many of these have become "nurse trees," with saplings growing in the rotten wood, all in a row.

Take a **whale watch and wildlife cruise** with Cross Sound Express (888-698-2726) to Point Adolphus and Icy Strait. The 3½-hour tour has two departures a day. Underwater microphones let you listen in on the songs of humpback whales. Orcas, harbor porpoises, Steller sea lions, and sea otters are frequently sighted.

Flightseeing trips over the Brady Ice Field and Fairweather Range are available with Air Excursions (907-697-2375) or L.A.B. Flying Service (907-789-9160). During an hour's excursion, the plane lands in front of a glacier or on a beach studded with aquamarine bergs.

Margerie Glacier, where you can see the first stage of the plant succession cycle.

■ LONGER OUTINGS

Because foot travel in the park is limited to beaches, moraines, and rocky avalanche chutes, **kayaking** is one of the best ways to explore. "Living with the tides" is the M.O. here. Squalls come and go; tarps are put up and taken down. Glacier Bay Sea Kayaking (907-697-2257; www.glacierbayseakayaks.com) rents both double and single kayaks. Kayaking in Icy Strait or Glacier Bay ranges from a half day to 14 days. A half-day guided trip is $50, including kayak.

Kayakers can guide themselves to the Beardslee Islands near Bartlett Cove for a day or overnight trip. Moose regularly swim to and from the Beardslees—and orcas sometimes nab a snack of moose. Campers are required to attend an orientation at the visitor information center before departure.

Most visitors make time for the all-day **tidewater glacier trip** on the park concession boat *Spirit of Adventure*, a stable catamaran that seats 200 in comfortable, heated decks. A Forest Service naturalist discusses all the sights, from seabird rookeries to sea otters. The boat stops near the Canadian border, swiveling back and forth between the 250-foot-high terminuses of the Margerie and Grand Pacific glaciers. The Grand Pacific grinds through softer rock, presenting a dirty face to the world. The Margerie is cleaner and whiter.

S I T K A

Sitka lies on the west side of Baranof Island, about 95 miles southwest of Juneau. Its name means "people on the outside of the island." Legend says that the Kiks.adi (the dot indicates a sound in the throat for which English has no consonant) Tlingit paddled here in prehistoric times seeking a village site, towing a wooden frog emblem behind one of their canoes. Sitka had all they needed: fish (especially a spring herring run), game, timber, berries, seaweed, and other resources.

Sitka's two harbors face more than a hundred evergreen-topped islands. To the west rises the cone of Mt. Edgecumbe, an extinct volcano often compared to Mt. Fuji because of its smooth conical shape. The ocean around here is an important summer feeding ground for whales, sea otters, and sea lions. The climate is mild, if damp—but Sitka still has many more sunny days than Juneau. It's a good place to explore on foot. Streets radiate out like spokes of a wheel from the picturesque Russian Orthodox church. Instead of lemonade, kids sell Russian wedding cookies from folding tables. Stroll along shady Lincoln Street, enjoying the breeze from Crescent Harbor, licking powdered sugar from your fingers—perfect!

■ SITKA THEN

Sitka's original inhabitants, the Kiks.adi Tlingit, established trading relationships with other nearby Native communities, using seagoing canoes to reach the Haida to the south and Copper River Ahtna to the north. The Spanish navigator Juan Perez may have been the first European to attempt to land near Sitka. In 1774 Perez bartered for fresh water with the Kiks.adi.

In the late 18th century the Russians moved in, under the command of the resilient, charismatic Alexander Baranof (1746–1819), the chief manager of the Russian-American Company. Russia hoped to control the trade in sea-otter pelts, and to that end began to extend its reach along the Alaskan coast. In 1799 Baranof led a flotilla of 300 kayaks and two ships south from Prince William Sound. Waves swallowed 30 kayaks en route, and there were skirmishes with the Kolosh. But Baranof pressed on, traveling at night. He was met at Sitka Sound by a large crowd of Kiks.adi and their chief, Skayeutlelt. Baranov bargained for land upon which to build a post, christened Archangel Michael (now Old Sitka).

SITKA, ALASKA - THE THREE SISTERS in the BACKGROUND

A trio of peaks overlooks Sitka, ca. the early 1900s.

Baranof described the Kiks.adi Tlingits as "numerous, strong and audacious." He and his men survived the winter and he departed the following spring, leaving a company of 450 people, mostly Aleut sea-otter hunters and their wives in a fortified garrison.

In June 1802 Skayeutlelt, egged on by his nephew Katlian, turned on the Russians in what is sometimes called the Sitka Massacre.

The Tlingit planned the attack carefully. Conspirators included Haida chiefs from the Queen Charlotte Islands, as well as Tlingit chiefs from five other tribes. On a Sunday afternoon, when some of the garrison men were fishing or berry picking, the warriors suddenly emerged from the forest armed with guns, spears, and daggers. One description of the battle claims there were over a thousand attackers. Of the 450 men, women, and children at the garrison, only 42 survived.

Baranof mobilized his forces. He returned in 1804 with a fleet of 300 kayaks, 800 Aleut hunters, 120 Russians, and 4 small ships. The *Neva,* a warship under the command of Urey Lisiansky, met him at Sitka Sound. Lisiansky had his cannon installed on a raft so they could get even closer to the Tlingit fortifications. At first the Tlingit seemed to hold their own. In a magnificent helmet, Katlian stalked the

Sitka is a mother lode of Native arts and crafts.

FAQs:

Why was Alaska called "Walrussia" and "Seward's Icebox" at the time of the purchase?

Although U.S. Secretary of State William Seward gave a three-hour speech to Congress describing the territory, outlining its peoples and desirable resources in some detail, newspapers treated its acquisition as a big joke. As a result, the general public became convinced that Alaska was a place of perpetual ice suitable only for Eskimos and walruses.

What is frybread?

Frybread is a Native American dish sometimes called "the Indian tortilla." It developed when flour, bread dough, and frying were introduced to Eskimo, Tlingit, Apache, and Navajo. It resembles pita or pocket bread, and is best served warm from the skillet. Pick up its scent at fairs and during holiday weekends. Frybread is often served drizzled with honey or topped with pinto beans, lettuce, tomato, and cheese for a hearty "Indian taco."

Why was Sitka called the "Paris of the North Pacific"?

From a rustic outpost, Sitka transformed itself into a cosmopolitan port where ships were built and launched. Particularly after 1840, when the talented linguist and inventor Bishop Ivan Veniaminov was in permanent residence, scholarly and scientific pursuits began to replace some of the rowdier fur-trader elements. The town had a library, a museum, a meteorological observatory, and a hospital. Balls were held, and wealthy ladies imported the finest fashions for such occasions.

Guests at a Sitka potlatch, ca. 1904.

beach wielding an iron blacksmith's hammer and a double-ended dagger. But gradually force of arms won out, and the surviving Tlingit escaped into the forest.

Baranof erected a new fort on the site of the vanquished Tlingit stronghold, later called "Castle Hill." He called it New Archangel. Conditions were bleak, and the men constantly manned the palisades, ready to repulse another attack. The deadlock continued until Baranof was about to retire in 1818, when Katlian came to bid him farewell. "Now we are old men together and about to die, let us be brothers," Katlian said.

Baranof knew he could not rid the region of competition from American traders. So he did the next best thing: he divvied up with them. In 1809 he made a share agreement with the Americans or "Boston men." Five years later he made a similar agreement with the Pacific Fur Company, owned by John Jacob Astor. As the town prospered, a barracks, a customs house, a Russian Orthodox seminary, two schools, and a governor's "castle" were built, and a foundry and sawmill began operating.

During its Russian heyday in the early 19th century, Sitka was the busiest port on the eastern shore of the Pacific, and the only shipyard north of Hawaii. It shipped ice from Swan Lake to San Francisco during the California Gold Rush.

MISSIONARIES AND BUSINESSMEN

Unlike the maritime fur traders, the missionaries and industrialists who arrived in the second half of the nineteenth century came to live on a long-term basis. They deliberately sought to influence the customs and beliefs of the Natives. The missionaries brought a new religion, schools and a new language. The businessmen brought a new economic system. Caucasian settlement of the Northwest Coast meant that new material goods were available to the Indians. . . . In some ways, the material standard of living increased greatly. However, to earn money to buy the goods, Indians had to take jobs and participate in the new economy. Whether or not they intended to work together, the missionaries and the businessmen influenced the Northwest Coast people in similar ways.

. . . missionaries sought to suppress the potlatch celebrations. Missionaries fought the potlatches for a number of reasons. They feared the drinking and the unsanitary conditions that began to characterize the celebrations after Caucasians introduced the Natives to alcohol. Employed Indians abandoned their jobs to participate in the potlatches. School attendance plummeted. Some missionaries felt that feasting Natives squandered food that they needed to hoard during the winter months. Finally, the potlatch played a strong role in passing myths and customs to the younger generation, and reinforced traditional economic and social structures.

—Victoria Wyatt, *Shapes of Their Thoughts: Reflections of Culture Contact in Northwest Coast Indian Art*, 1984

The administrative headquarters for Russian America followed Baranof from Kodiak to Sitka. While all this high living was taking place on one side of the stockade, on the other side the Tlingit lived in rough conditions, facing a battery of eight Russian cannon.

Little changed for the Kiks.adi, according to authors Richard and Nora Dauenhauer. "The Russians . . . were not strong enough to undertake a full-scale occupation of Tlingit country," they write in *Haa Kusteeyí, Our Culture*, "and the areas beyond the fort at Sitka remained in Tlingit control. . . . For the most part, the traditional Tlingit social system remained intact, and the Tlingit were not disturbed in their traditional use of the land and its resources." But for many years, diseases such as smallpox tore through the Tlingit population.

Tlingit crafts registered the social shift. Instead of large burden baskets and hats of cedar bark and spruce root, weavers began turning out souvenir items such as recycled wine and medicine bottles covered with basketry. Rather than working in copper, Tlingit artisans hammered silver dollars into brooches, bracelets, and spoons, some decorated with the American eagle from the coin itself rather than traditional split, two-dimensional, symmetrical "form line" designs.

Bishop Ivan Veniaminov, who visited Sitka in 1834 and settled there in 1840, made major strides in converting Natives to Christianity. He made efforts to develop a writing system for various Native languages, introducing Natives to the Russian Orthodox teachings but also, in the end, helping to preserve these oral languages. For schoolchildren in Sitka, he prepared bilingual textbooks himself, with parallel texts in Tlingit and Russian. He also urged vaccinations against Western diseases. (Vaccination and conversion often went hand in hand.)

As the sea-otter-pelt trade waned, Russia approached the United States with an offer to sell its Alaskan land. The agreement was signed in Washington, D.C., on March 30, 1867. The Americans took formal possession on October 18, 1867, during a ceremony on Sitka's Castle Hill, as the town became the capital of the United States' new Alaska Territory. A Navy man, C.D. Bloodgood, reported on the immediate influx of opportunists: "Before our first sunset gun was fired, their preempting stakes dotted the ground, and ere long they had framed a city charter, devised laws and remunerative offices, and by an election, at which less than one hundred votes were mustered, gave publicity to, and inaugurated their schemes. Their squatter claims were confirmed and recorded." The Tlingit were not permitted into Sitka to witness the transfer ceremonies. They could only stand on the beach beyond the palisade in their separate village, the "Ranche."

Administration of "Seward's Icebox" was turned over to the War Department, with an artillery regiment dispatched to keep order. The regiment established garrisons at Sitka, Wrangell, and Tongass. For decades, the only law in Alaska consisted of orders issued to the Commanding General. He was directed to "impress upon the Indians and especially upon their chiefs, that our government will regard them as subject to its laws and entitled to its protection; that while they are protected by our government they will be required to respect the rights of all citizens

(right, at top) The Cathedral of the Archangel Michael speaks to the 19th-century Russian community. (right, at bottom) The view down Lincoln Street in the early 1900s. Native women selling souvenirs have set up shop under the trees.

of the republic." In other words, Native Americans were not citizens. To be considered for citizenship, they were required to lead a "civilized life"—a term interpreted variously by the authorities.

Jefferson Davis, Commanding General in 1867, visited Tlingit and Haida villages, warning the residents against molesting white men. Before these meetings, some Natives had been aware of the sale of Alaska and objected to the transaction on the grounds that the Russians had no right to sell Tlingit land.

In 1878 John Green Brady arrived in Sitka as a missionary, staying to become a businessman and politician. As the fifth governor of the District of Alaska, Brady collected 15 Haida totem poles and a 54-foot war canoe for the Alaska exhibit at the Louisiana Purchase Exposition held in St. Louis in 1904 and the Lewis and Clark Exposition in Portland a year later. The poles became the basis for Sitka National Monument.

Sitka hummed along quietly until Pearl Harbor. The Navy then fortified Japonski Island, building a base there with 30,000 military personnel. This had a huge impact on both the culture and economy of the town. Today the U.S. Coast Guard maintains facilities on Japonski, and the island has been connected with the mainland by a bridge. The major postwar economic player was the Alaska Lumber and Pulp Company. Its main timber facility closed in 1993—another shock from which the town is still recovering.

■ SITKA NOW *map page 155*

Unlike many Alaskan towns, Sitka brims with history—Tlingit, Russian, Alaskan. The town's architectural centerpiece is the 19th-century Russian Orthodox cathedral at the head of Lincoln Street. The historic centerpiece is Sitka National Historical Park, established in 1910 to commemorate the 1804 Battle of Sitka. Its 113 acres include a visitors center and the Southeast Alaska Indian Cultural Center, as well as the site of the Tlingit fort and battlefield, the Russian Bishop's House, a memorable loop trail lined with totems, and a memorial to the Russian midshipmen who died in the battle.

The Tlingit "Ranche" has still not been completely absorbed into the "Russian side" of downtown, an example of the enduring tensions between Natives and non-Natives throughout Alaska. The Alaska Native Claims Settlement Act of 1971 helped to bridge the economic gap to some degree, but grudges and prejudices simmer not far beneath the surface on both sides.

KID STUFF

■ Bring crayons. A junior ranger activity book about Sitka National Historical Park is available to children 4 and up at the park's visitors center (106 Metlakatla Street; 907-747-6281).

■ Visit a wild bird hospital, the Alaska Raptor Center (1101 Sawmill Creek Road; 907-747-8662; www.alaskaraptor.org), where injured bald eagles, golden eagles, hawks, owls, and falcons are rehabilitated. The eye-dazzler here is the 20,000-square-foot flight-training center, designed to look like rain forest. You can watch exercising birds through one-way glass. The center is an easy 10-minute walk from Sitka National Historical Park.

Although residents may not agree on every issue, Sitka's strong-minded population (just under 9,000 in 2004) values the town's history. Putting the beauty of their waterfront ahead of commercial development, residents have opposed a downtown cruise-ship dock. As a result, at this writing all cruise-ship passengers are tendered to shore.

■ WALKING TOUR

Starting where cruise-ship passengers come ashore, on Harbor Drive near the O'Connell Bridge, head into town on Harbor. You can make a detour to the left to see Castle Hill, or see it on the way back.

Make a left on Observatory Street to reach the domed **Cathedral of the Archangel Michael** (Lincoln and Seward streets; 907-747-8120), sitting regally in its own little circle of streets. Under the direction of Veniaminov, its foundation was laid in 1848, in the shape of a cross. The vaulted interior is laid out in the Orthodox manner, with the sanctuary separated from the public area by a gilded screen called an iconostasis. This partition is adorned with 12 icons with silver adornments. The central door leading to the sanctuary is called the Royal Gates; through this ceremonial portal the Eucharist is brought out to the faithful. What visitors see today is a reconstruction; the cathedral suffered a fire in 1966. However, the present structure was built from the plans of the original, and residents managed to save many antique religious items now on display.

A TLINGIT SAMPLER

Wasa-i-yatee (pronounced *wasa-ee-ya-tee*): "How are you?"

Yak'ei (*yuk-ay*): "Good."

Ax-xooni (*ach-hoonee*): "My friend."

Igu-ayax-xwan (*ee-gooayug-won*): "Be brave."

Gunalcheesh (*gun-nush-cheesh*): "Thank you."

Hit (*hit*): Clan house, as in Yehlh hit, "Raven's House."

Dis or disi (*disee*): month or moon, as in Tahwak disi, "goose moon."

Keet (*keet*): killer whale.

Sha (*sha*): mountains.

Xoots or Hootz (*kootz*): brown bear; or as in the proper name Anna Hootz, "Brown bear country," a Ka-gwan-tan chief's name at Sitka

Kootznoowoo (*kootz-nu-wu*): "Fortress of the brown bears." The name for Admiralty Island.

Woosh-Jee-Een (*woosh-jee-een*): "Working Together." The motto of the Huna Heritage Foundation, the non-profit arm of the native corporation of the village of Hoonah.

Hoonah (*who-nah*): "The place where the north wind doesn't blow."

From the cathedral, walk along Lincoln Street to the **Sitka Convention & Visitors Bureau** (upstairs, 303 Lincoln Street; 907-747-5940; www.sitka.org), where you can get information about all local attractions. Then continue along Lincoln about two blocks to the **Russian Bishop's House** (Lincoln and Baranof streets; 907-747-6281). This is a rarity—one of only four original colonial Russian structures remaining in North America. The two-story log structure, built in 1843, contains the refurbished quarters of Bishop Veniaminov with a private chapel. (Veniaminov was canonized by the Orthodox Church as St. Innocent.) Exhibits illustrate the Russian fur trade in Alaska and the roles of the Russian-American Company and Russian Orthodox Church. It's open by appointment only.

Get a handle on how Sitka looked under Russian rule by viewing the model town at the **Isabel Miller Museum** in the Harrigan Centennial Building (330 Harbor Drive; 907-747-6455). The museum focuses on the shared history of Russian, American, and Tlingit residents. On the grounds is a 50-foot replica of a Tlingit war canoe.

The **Sheldon Jackson Museum** stands at a seeming driveway that is at right angles to Lincoln Street, on the Sheldon Jackson College campus. Built in 1895, the museum (104 College Drive; 907-747-8981; www.museums.state.ak.us) displays the state's oldest continuously exhibited collection of Alaska Native art and artifacts, including shamans' gear and totems. The eponymous missionary-educator Reverend Dr. Jackson gathered his collection between 1888 and 1898. His museum was the first fireproof and the first concrete structure in Alaska. One treasure is the helmet that Katlian, the Tlingit war leader, wore during the battle of 1804. It is carved from a knot of wood covered with bearskin and topped with a raven whose eyes are inlaid with copper. Also investigate the drawers with glass lids that hold special treasures such as children's toys from several cultures. The attached store is a great place to shop for jewelry and crafts—objects an aesthetic cut or two above "souvenirs."

The walk so far would take about four hours. If you still have stamina, press on around the curve of Lincoln Street to Sitka National Historical Park, about an eighth of a mile away (*see* Brief Excursions).

■ BRIEF EXCURSIONS

Explore **Sitka National Historical Park** (end of Lincoln Street; 907-747-6281; www.nps.gov/sitk/), a 113-acre preserve that includes the site of the Tlingit fort and the 1804 battle with the Russians. Outside the visitors center's front door are large contemporary totems that record Tlingit history. Inside the visitors center is the **Southeast Alaska Indian Cultural Center,** which includes both a museum and workshops. During the summer you can watch Native craftspeople beading, making jewelry, and carving wood. The 10-minute slide show *Battle of Sitka* helps explain precisely what happened here in 1804. Exit the back door and take the self-guided tour along a one-mile wooded path, where spruce trees arch overhead and ravens evermore yawp in the branches. Totem poles are spaced along this path—a favorite with locals. (The forest trail is wheelchair accessible.) The rocky shore of Sitka Sound paralleling the totem path is a pleasant place for a picnic.

Koo.eex'—that is, welcome to a ceremony at which both Eagles and Ravens will be in attendance. The tall panels flanking the entrance to the **Sheet'ka Kwaan Naa Kahidi Tribal House** (200 Katlian Street; 907-747-7137) represent the Eagle and

(following pages) There's no missing Mt. Edgecumbe, an extinct volcano.

THE TONGASS

The Tongass National Forest is 17 million acres of green, the largest national forest in the United States. Set aside in 1907, the preserve—approximately the size of West Virginia—encompasses about 90 percent of Southeast Alaska.

Under the management of the U.S. Forest Service, it has been designated "multiple use." Rather than being reserved solely for logging *or* mining, it is used for logging *and* mining, plus recreation. Greenpeace regularly anchors one of its larger ships in ports along the Inside Passage and gives visitors tours and information about the issues involved in forest management. It's a contentious issue. Small Alaskan towns need jobs, and lobby for logging. Residents of larger towns criticize the way clearcut forests look and how long it takes them to recover.

The cool, damp, temperate rain forest of the Tongass supports species such as red and yellow cedar, western hemlock, and Sitka spruce. Resistant to insects, Sitka spruce can live to be 700 years old and 200 feet tall. Native peoples harvested Sitka spruce logs to build their plank houses, totems, and canoes, and to carve paddles, bowls, and storage boxes. They also gathered spruce roots and bark for weaving and used devil's club (a thorny plant related to ginseng) for medicine.

The early Russian emigrants harvested trees at Sitka to build ships. When steamships carried tourists to Alaska, they took on firewood that was cut in what is today the Tongass. Those logged-over areas have grown back. During World War I spruce was requisitioned by the military to build aircraft. In World War II spruce was used for gliders. Little wholesale logging took place until after World War II.

But the Tongass is not just trees. It also includes glaciers, mountains, lakes, islands, straits, and channels. And there is an exceptional abundance of wildlife here. Bald eagles make the Tongass their home. Black and brown bears live here, as do Sitka black-tailed deer, mountain goats, beavers, lynx, wolves, wolverines, red foxes, river otters, great blue herons, little brown bats, porcupines, martens, the northern goshawk, the marbled murrelet, red and flying squirrels, and weasels. Both saltwater and freshwater fish flourish here too, including five species of salmon.

From Tongass gateway towns such as Ketchikan or Sitka you can take self-guided hikes, bike tours, or guided Jeep excursions on back roads. A sojourn at a remote cabin is a way to get up-close-and-dazzled. The Tongass has 145 cabins for public use, 80 of them accessible from Ketchikan. For information, contact the Forest Supervisor in Ketchikan (907-225-3101), Sitka (907-747-6671), Juneau (907-586-8751), or Petersburg (907-772-3841).

Raven moieties. Drummers set the beat and a songleader gives the commands, as dancers in outfits of deerskin, felt, feathers, and intricate beadwork circle the floor. Some dancers wear frontlets (masks at forehead level) or face-covering masks, while others twirl and stomp in Chilkat blankets or button blankets. Their dress—not "costumes"—may include *at.oow*, colorful regalia showing clan crests. Performances are given against a backdrop of two carved house screens, giving a strong impression of what a potlatch celebration would have looked like in the late 1800s. The 30-minute dances are scheduled mostly in summer.

■ LONGER OUTINGS

Saltwater fishing is high on many must-do lists, especially since statistically the chances of hooking into a king are excellent. Saltwater angling is at its best June through August. The most common catches are king, silver, and pink salmon, halibut, and ling cod. A list of charter operators is available from the Convention & Visitors Bureau (907-747-5940).

You can arrange for a three-hour **wildlife-spotting harbor tour** with Annahootz Alaskan Adventures, in search of sea lions, humpbacks, sea otters, and brown bears (907-747-2608; www.annahootz.com).

For a more leisurely time, try **a week-long wilderness tour** on a converted commercial vessel with Coastal Wilderness Adventures (800-287-7063; www.homeshore.com). The ship is equipped with kayaks (beginners welcome) for exploring the shoreline up close or venturing into the Chichagof Wilderness.

Board Alaska's only semi-submersible tour vessel to **get an underwater look at Sitka Sound** with Sea Life Discovery Tours (877-966-2301; www.greenlingenterprises.com). Jellyfish, waving forests of kelp, anemones, and sea stars are common sights. Trips are available for either 1½ or 2 hours.

PRACTICAL INFORMATION

■ ANIMAL- AND BIRD-WATCHING

It's a good idea to learn a bit about habitat, animal behavior, and migratory patterns so that you'll know what to look for. If you have questions about particular species, get in touch with the Forest Service Information Center in Juneau (907-586-8751; www.fs.fed.us/r10/Tongass). Whether you're stalking falcons or seals, bring a pair of binoculars. (Some cruises and tours, as in Glacier Bay National Park, will supply them for the length of the trip.) Local guides and boat skippers are generally adept at spotting game and will point animals and birds out to you, then maneuver as close as allowable. The most basic rule of thumb is, of course, be patient.

You can check the Web site WildLifeWatcher.com for info on the best time to visit specific sites to increase your odds of sighting moose, bears, and other creatures. Birdzilla.com offers bird touring information.

■ BEARS

Black and brown (grizzly) bears can be seen from May through September near food sources such as avalanche chutes, berry patches, and salmon-spawning areas. In these months bears leave forest cover to take advantage of spawning salmon. Boaters often spot them in Misty Fiords, Tracy Arm, and Glacier Bay, as well as at Anan Creek near Wrangell and Pack Creek in the Stan Price State Wildlife Sanctuary 30 miles south of Juneau. In August and September the banks of the Chilkoot River near Haines are another reliable sighting spot. Since fall 2002, brown bears and cubs have been frequenting some trails near Juneau's Mendenhall Glacier Visitors Center. Bears also hit the beaches to nibble on kelp or go clamming. The least invasive way to watch animals, including bears, is to book a charter with a boat captain who knows where to find them grazing on beaches. For example, Alaska Discovery (907-780-6226; www.akdiscovery.com), offers bear-viewing kayak trips at Admiralty Island.

■ WHALES, SEALS, AND PORPOISES

About 750 humpback whales migrate annually to the Inside Passage and can be viewed April through September. Their breathing can be heard at great distances, and this distinctive sound often reveals their presence. These huge, acrobatic mammals travel in pods of six to eight, taking shallow dives. They're often seen near Juneau and Admiralty Island, especially in passes and narrows along their migration routes. Trying to photograph a solitary humpback can be daunting, because the average breach lasts just three seconds. A pod increases your chance of capturing the action.

Orcas (killer whales), minke whales, and porpoises may be sighted too. Orca pods follow salmon runs, so peak viewing periods are April through September. Orcas are able to "spyhop," or pop their heads vertically out of the water without actually leaping. Both orcas and minkes can be seen in Glacier Bay and Frederick Sound. The Pacific white-sided dolphin is commonly spotted near Ketchikan. Both the Harbor porpoise and the Dall's porpoise are common in Southeast Alaska. The Harbor porpoise swims close to shore, but is shy and dives frequently. Dall's porpoises enjoy riding the bow waves of boats and may travel in groups. You can tell them apart by the way Dall's porpoises may jump or spin out of the water. (Harbor porpoises don't.)

Harbor seals may be seen year-round. Their pupping areas include Tracy Arm Fjord south of Juneau and Glacier Bay. When seals are pupping in May and June, waters near pupping haul-outs (reefs, beaches, and icebergs) are often closed to tour boats so that birthing and nursing continue undisturbed. Harbor seals are usually solitary, so if you see groups of "something" in the water spyhopping to look at you, you're probably seeing Steller sea lions. There are rookeries of Steller sea lions near Juneau, Gustavus and Ketchikan.

Keep in mind that laws protect whales from ship traffic. Boats are not to approach closer than 100 yards. It's also forbidden to feed sea lions and other creatures. Substantial fines await vessel skippers or others found guilty of such practices. Whale-watching tour operators may offer "100% sightings guaranteed." Such a guarantee may lead a captain to ignore the law. When choosing a tour operator, ask how long the captain has conducted such tours; this will give you an indication of his or her expertise.

■ Birds

Let's not neglect our avian neighbors. Each bald eagle requires about a mile of shoreline for feeding; this means eagles perch in trees along the Inside Passage at regular intervals. They particularly favor tall, dead trees as lookouts, but may also use wharf posts and steeples. The Alaska Chilkat Bald Eagle Preserve outside

Haines is the best place to see eagles, but raptor centers in Sitka and Juneau are also good bets. It's against the law to "chum," or throw fish scraps into the water to lure eagles closer. Doing so will net the guilty party a heavy fine.

Rufous hummingbirds, the crested Steller's Jay (with blue wings and tail), and Canada geese are other common species along the Inside Passage. The Dusky Canada goose commutes year-round to Juneau's Mendenhall Wetlands. And you'll see ravens doing their hokey-pokey near fast-food joints and supermarkets as they hunt for scraps.

■ ANIMAL SAFETY

Most wild animals have no desire to cross your path—but they should be warned of human presence so that you don't startle them. When hiking where visibility is limited by terrain or weather, **make noise.** Talk, sing, or whistle; if you have a trekking pole, knock it against rocks. **Don't try to feed animals** or leave out food to attract them for close-up pictures.

You won't need to worry about snakes or poisonous spiders—there aren't any in Alaska. Wolves are rarely seen. Never approach Steller sea lions or seals; they're protected.

■ BEARS

If you suddenly see a bear, it may perceive the place where you're standing as its right-of-way. Wave your arms to appear larger. Clap your hands. Speak to the bear. Never approach the bear and **never run away.** (Bears can easily outrun humans.) Stand your ground, or back up slowly. Bears, like most omnivores, consider anything fleeing as fair game. Never get between a sow and her cub. If you see a cub and not the sow, back away quietly. A brown bear's sense of smell is 100,000 times as acute as a human's, so don't piggyback a deer carcass. If you're camping, be sure to use airtight containers for food and do your cooking away from your site. Don't bring any food or anything that smells like food into your tent—even a chocolate bar can bring a grizz nuzzling up. For more advice on safety around bears, check the Alaska Department of Fish & Game Web site, www.adfg.state.ak.us.

■ MOOSE

Moose are totally unpredictable. If you run across one, it can retreat, its huge bulk quickly disappearing ghost-like in the brush—or it might advance at a trot to stomp on you. There are no moose in most of Southeast Alaska. However, in the Gustavus forelands there is an estimated density of 3.8 moose per square kilometer, and sometimes moose outnumber humans two to one. If you do happen to see a moose on a trail, do not try to go around it. Wait 5 or 10 minutes to see if the moose moves. If it does not, retreat slowly and quietly. Like most protective moms, moose with calves will do their utmost to protect them from perceived danger, so you should be particularly careful if you see any calves.

■ ANTIQUITIES LAWS

After decades of unauthorized grave-robbing, Alaska takes its antiquities very seriously. The maximum fine is $250,000 and 10 years in jail.

Alaska's first antiquities laws went on the books in 1906. Rock hounds will be pleased to note, however, that it is permissible to collect small samples of ancient plant and invertebrate (snail, clam, etc.) fossils in most parts of the state, including the entire Inside Passage. No samples collected can be sold. On the other hand, unless you have a permit issued for scientific research, you may not collect or move

Mountain goats scrambling in Glacier Bay National Park.

any prehistoric or historic artifacts such as arrowheads, prospectors' boot soles on the Chilkoot Trail, old bottles, mining equipment, or human remains. Anyone stumbling upon dinosaur fossils is asked to notify authorities of their location. Petroglyphs (ancient markings on rock) are similarly protected.

■ BOATING

Waking up anchored in a quiet cove and watching porpoises chase fish while you sip coffee is one of Alaska's most delightful experiences. Chartering a sailboat is one way to do this. If you wish to charter a boat with captain, visitors centers can supply lists of recommended outfits.

Kayaks and power boats can be rented in most towns, with instruction thrown in. If you're new to kayaking, the best way to get comfortable is to take a guided tour before going it alone.

Taking a dip in Metlakatla.

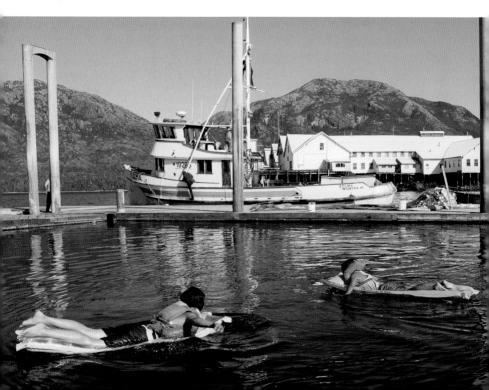

The quieter the craft you use, the more likely you are to spot wildlife on the beach before it spots you, or to experience the thrill of having a curious harbor seal trail you. Guided tours on inflatable rafts can supply the heady excitement of rapids as well as plenty of scenery. Float trips are available out of most Inside Passage ports, and you can even paddle a traditional Tlingit canoe with Auk Ta Shaa Discovery (800-820-2628; www.goldbelttours.com). Adventures Afloat (800-3-AFLOAT), based in Juneau, offers personalized multi-day adventures on the 106-foot *Valkyrie* and 32-foot *High Roller*.

On the other hand, if speed and loud engines are your cup of tea, take a jet-boat tour. Breakaway Adventures offers jet boats out of Wrangell to the Stikine River, Anan Bear Observatory, and the Shakes and LeConte glaciers (888-385-2488; www.breakawayadventures.com). Alaska Vistas (866-874-3006) offers rafting trips of the Stikine River as well as guided kayak expeditions. Absolutely Alaskan/Yeshua Guided Tours offers jet boats in the Haines and Skagway areas (907-766-2334).

Sailors should note the "Spirit of Adventure-Around Admiralty" race, starting from Juneau's Auke Bay in mid-June. The 200-mile sailboat race is billed as the longest inland-water sailing race in the Pacific Northwest. The possibility of icebergs in Tracy Arm is just part of the fun.

■ CLIMATE

On a brief visit to Juneau in 1935, humorist Will Rogers was asked why he was buying two raincoats. "If I were staying longer, I'd buy three," Rogers replied.

The Inside Passage is a maritime "road" surrounded by rain forest. So you'll need to equip yourself with a sturdy raincoat with attached hood or a folding umbrella. (Many cruise-ship lines distribute poncho-like raingear—essentially giant trash bags with neck and arm holes—which give scant protection.)

Down coats are unnecessary unless you chronically suffer from chilly extremities. Daytime summer temperatures range from 44 to 85 degrees Fahrenheit. Fifty-five degrees and cloudy is typical. It is rare for the temperature to rise above 70°F in Juneau, although several new records were set during the summer of 2004. The shoulder season is usually more blustery and chillier—hardy sightseers send home damp postcards logging the wind speed.

■ CLOTHING

Alaskans don shorts when the mercury reaches 55°F, but many visitors wrap up in down at that temperature. To best prepare for changing temperatures, dress in layers of synthetics with a fleece vest. Sidewalks tend to be uneven or non-existent, so backless shoes, flimsy sandals, and high heels are risky. Sturdy lace-up walking shoes suffice for most exploration, except extended forays into the backcountry. Don't fret about your appearance; most Alaskans totally ignore high fashion.

Bound for a flightseeing tour featuring a glacier landing? Dress warmly with hat and gloves, and bring sunglasses to cut the glare of light from ice and water.

For fishing excursions, knee-high rubber boots are de rigueur, because you may need to wade to the boat, depending on the docking facilities. A hat with a brim all around helps to cut the glare; it should have a chinstrap so that the wind can't kidnap it. Kayaking tour operators typically provide waterproof suits and boots as well as flotation vests.

Be prepared with a fleece hat, gloves, and scarf on day cruises, in mine tunnels, at outdoor theater performances, when whale- or bird-watching, golfing, beach-combing, dog sledding, or on float trips.

■ FESTIVALS AND ANNUAL EVENTS

Although most visitors tour the Inside Passage between May and September, special events and celebrations punctuate the entire year. Here is a sampling of some of the best.

January

The Alcan 200 Road Rally is a snow-machine race from the U.S./Canada border near Haines to Dezadeash Lake and back. The Polar Bear Dip on New Year's Day in Juneau brings out the hardy—and the shivering.

February

During the first weekend of this month, Wrangell's Tent City Days re-create some of the spirit of the 19th-century gold rushes with competitions like beard-growing and tall-tales contests. At the Shady Lady Fancy Dress Ball, women show off their décolletages.

The Children of All Nations Dancers wait to begin a performance in Juneau.

March

The Gold Medal Basketball Tournament brings teams from all over the state to Juneau. The teams of elders compete as if their lives depended on it.

April

Mendenhall Golf Course, 10 miles from downtown Juneau, opens for play. Juneau's Folk Festival offers musical headliners from around the region. Ketchikan celebrates the Alaska Hummingbird Festival.

May

The Little Norway Festival in Petersburg celebrates Norwegian Constitution Day with everything from Viking raids to halibut-filleting contests. Wrangell, Sitka, Ketchikan, and Petersburg all host salmon derbies. Haines celebrates regional microbrews at its Great Alaska Craftbeer & Homebrew Festival.

June

Bicyclists drool over the Annual Kluane to Chilkat Bike Relay, from Haines Junction, Yukon Territory, to the Fort Seward parade grounds in Haines, Alaska. The course is 160 miles through spectacular Kluane Park and the Alaska Chilkat Bald Eagle Preserve. Juneau celebrates Gold Rush Days with logging and mining events. Sitka's Summer Music Festival attracts world-famous musicians.

July

Soapy Smith's Wake in Skagway toasts the infamous con man every July 8. Ketchikan stages its *Fish Pirate's Daughter* melodrama, and Prince of Wales Island puts on its Logging Show & Fair (www.princeofwalescoc.org). All Inside Passage towns whoop it up on the Fourth of July in a big way with parades, marching bands, and canoe races. Because of competition from the midnight sun, Juneau's Fourth of July fireworks display begins about 11:30 P.M. on July 3.

August

Juneau holds its 60th annual Golden North Salmon Derby in 2006. There are significant cash prizes as well as prizes for catching tagged fish. The annual Blueberry Arts Festival in Ketchikan includes a pie-eating contest. Haines hosts the annual Southeast Alaska State Fair, showcasing local activities with events like a logging show and a fiddle contest.

September
The Klondike Road Relay, a 110-mile race, kicks off in Skagway and ends in Whitehorse. Sitka holds its Labor Day Weekend Mudball Classic Softball Tournament.

October
Sitka honors Alaska Day on the 18th, the anniversary of formal ceremonies marking the purchase of Alaska from Russia. Festivities continue for several days and include a costume ball. Petersburg's Gallery Walk is part of a month of special events.

November
Haines toasts its eagles with the Alaska Bald Eagle Festival (www.baldeaglefest.org). Sitka begins Holiday Fest, which continues through January.

December
Sitka launches its Christmas Boat Parade. Juneau's Gallery Walk highlights visiting and resident artists. Haines ushers in the winter holidays with a Snow Dragon Parade.

■ FISHING

Along the Inside Passage there's little "combat fishing"—fishing shoulder-to-shoulder with a hundred others. Here you can charter a vessel to take you away from all that, to show you the captain's favorite reefs or halibut holes.

But don't expect to hook onto a big one on your first cast. By interviewing fishermen, the Alaska Department of Fish & Game keeps a running total of the hours an average marine boat angler needed to land each species. For example, a five-year average for catching coho salmon in the Juneau area is four hours. However, during the week of August 29 to September 5, 2004, it took five hours. In that same week, landing a halibut took 27 hours—although it was 8 hours the previous week.

Runs occur during different weeks in different parts of the Inside Passage. In general, kings (the largest salmon and Alaska's state fish) spawn in the spring and finish by mid-summer; sockeye, chum, and pink follow the king run; acrobatic silvers are available in August and September. For availability of halibut, Dolly Varden, rockfish and other species, consult a fishing guide. Because of global warming, new species sometimes venture into these waters.

If you're dreaming of something off the beaten track, consider a fishing "escape" in a remote location. Icy Strait Point opened to cruise ships in 2004, making it the newest destination port in Alaska. The original settlement here was a salmon cannery built in 1912. It was restored and modified to include a restaurant, a fishing history museum, and shops. Salmon and halibut are the fish to catch here. Icy Point is 20 minutes by air from Juneau. For details, contact Icy Strait Lodge (866-645-3636; www.icystraitlodge.com).

In Sitka you can fish for smelt in May and early June from the steel bridge over the Taiya River, at milepost 5.7 on the Dyea Road.

For fishing around the capital or to learn bag and possession limits, visit http://juneaualaska.com/fishing, or call the Division of Sport Fish (907-465-4270) or the Fishing Hotline (907-465-4116).

Non-resident sport-fishing licenses and king salmon stamps ($10 extra) are sold at many marine supply outlets and even some drugstores. To purchase a license online, go to www.admin.adfg.state.ak.us/license. Children under 16 do not need a license.

How big is a trophy? The king salmon averages 15 to 50 pounds; 50 pounds or over is considered a trophy. A "barn door" halibut is anything over 100 pounds—and always female. A rainbow trout 10 pounds or more, grayling 3 pounds, and red salmon 12 pounds are also trophy. During summer months, most towns hold fishing derbies with impressive cash prizes; for an extra fillip to your fishing trip, enter a contest such as Wrangell's King Salmon Derby (mid-May to mid-June). The top prize is $6,000.

■ FLIGHTSEEING

If you enjoy flying low enough to see swans on their nests, bush planes offer an exhilarating look at the landscape. Operators usually have scheduled tour itineraries, but may also be willing to take you wherever you wish to go. Be aware, however, that weather fronts can quickly reduce visibility and change everyone's plans.

TEMSCO Helicopters (877-789-9501; www.temscoair.com) developed Alaska's first glacier helicopter tour in 1983. Their offerings are representative of options here, as many flightseeing operators schedule similar flights. They operate out of Wrangell, Juneau, and Skagway. All tours include narration, and most are in A-star turbine helicopters known for their quiet ride and unobstructed views from every seat.

From Wrangell, one TEMSCO tour whisks you up the Stikine River and gives a good look at the tidewater LeConte Glacier. From Skagway, the Valley of the Glaciers flight lands at the base of a glacier. This flight is a more intimate experience than passing over an ice field; you'll get up close and personal with canyons and dramatic peaks. From Juneau, one popular trip includes views of the Juneau Ice Field and gives you 20 to 25 minutes with a mountaineering guide on the glacier surface. (Boots with good traction are provided.) Another Juneau option pairs a flight with a landing at a dog camp to try mushing—driving or riding in the sled.

In addition to TEMSCO, Wings of Alaska, L.A.B. Flying Service, Promech Air, Haines Airways, and other fly-boys serve the Inside Passage.

Note: Due to weight and balance restrictions, passengers weighing 250 pounds or more are sometimes charged an additional half-fare to reserve helicopter space.

■ Food

Although fresh seafood is ubiquitous in summer, few people come to the Inside Passage for the food. Adventure here lies not in the dining room but in gliding past icebergs close enough to hear them drip. Chefs tend to change frequently, so quality may not be consistent from year to year and menus often fluctuate.

Alaska has scant agriculture, so many basic ingredients—fresh herbs, corn, citrus fruit, beef, free-range chicken—must be flown or barged in. So ask about the catch of the day and hope it won't be overcooked. On the other hand, North Slope reindeer, Delta Junction buffalo, Kachemak Bay mussels, or Matanuska Valley carrots may be in season; look for these on local menus or inquire. If you're preparing for an alfresco meal, stop by a local bakery, market, or takeout for anything from bright green seaweed salad to cranberry muffins.

■ Ann's Favorite Restaurants

Unless otherwise noted, these choices are open year-round.

Ketchikan
New York Hotel & Café. A "coffee shop" holds the fort from 6 to 10 A.M. Then the focus switches to crab, shrimp, and other fresh seafood. The café sponsors the annual Trout Fishing in America Poetry Slam in August. *207 Stedman Street, Ketchikan; 907-225-0246. Closed October-April.*

WestCoast Cape Fox Lodge. This luxurious, modern lodge has one of only three eateries in Alaska reached by tram. Hotel guests and locals board free; others pay $2. Watch the lights of historic downtown while you dine. Specialties include halibut Olympia (baked with Bermuda onions) and seafood chowder. *800 Venetia Avenue, Ketchikan; 907-225-8001.*

Petersburg

Rooney's Northern Lights Restaurant. This spot, overlooking the harbor, serves three meals a day, daily-changing menus. Seafood is all, of course, a strong point with entrees like shrimp quesadillas and halibut wraps. If you've had it with fish you can dig into a juicy burger or steak. *203 Sing Lee Alley, Petersburg; 907-772-2900.*

Juneau

Chinook's. Two standout dishes here are the Shelter Island halibut and the pistachio crème brûlée. Breakfast is served until 2 P.M. Monday through Saturday; Sunday brings an all-you-can-eat brunch. *Goldbelt Hotel, 51 Egan Drive, Juneau; 888-478-6909.*

Douglas Café. Voted the source of Juneau's best burger. Summer specialties include Cajun-style halibut and salmon. *916 Third Street, Douglas Island; 907-364-3307. Limited hours October-April.*

The Fiddlehead Restaurant and Bakery. Known for its soups and breads, the Fiddlehead has been going strong since 1978. You can eat in the casual restaurant downstairs (focaccia sandwiches, pastas, and the like) or in the more formal, Italian-oriented **Di Sopra** upstairs. Di Sopra dishes up fresh ravioli daily. It has been called the "best eatery in Alaska" in the *New York Times* and has won a *Wine Spectator* Award of excellence. *429 West Willoughby Avenue, Juneau; 907-586-3150.*

The Gold Room. If you yearn to shed your pile jacket for an evening of roast pheasant, this is the place. Prime rib is often on the menu, but ask about seasonal tasting menus. It's not just a local favorite; the Gold Room is known throughout the state. *Westmark Baranof Hotel, 127 N. Franklin Street, Juneau; 907-586-2660.*

Taku Glacier Lodge. Combine peeks at peaks with a meal in a three-hour trip departing from downtown Juneau. The Wings Airways floatplane excursion includes views of five glaciers and a king salmon dinner at a 1920s log lodge. *907-586-8258. Closed October-April.*

Thane Ore House Salmon Bake. Make the trek to this beachfront spot for all-you-can-eat alder-grilled king or sockeye salmon, beer-battered halibut, and barbecued beef ribs. The space is decorated with mining memorabilia. There's a shuttle available from downtown Juneau. *4400 Thane Road; 907-586-3442. Closed September-April.*

Skagway

Stowaway Café. The Stowaway haggles directly with local fishermen in order to serve the freshest seafood possible. One sample dish is wasabi salmon, topped with panko crumbs and broiled. The café is also known for its daily baked bread and homemade soup. *205 Congress Way, Skagway; 907-983-3463. Closed October-April.*

Haines

Hotel Halsingland. Started by Swedish immigrants following World War II, this relaxed restaurant fills a historic Victorian building on Fort Seward. Top draws include its potato bar and fresh seafood dishes such as blackened salmon and crab dip served with house-made Parmesan-fennel crackerbread. Before your meal, sip a Fort Seward Howitzer in the lounge to set the mood. *The parade grounds, Haines; 907-766-2000.*

Rounding up pints at Skagway's Red Onion Saloon.

Sitka

Ludvig's Bistro Inc. The menu reflects co-owner Collette Nelson's apprentice-ships in Pacific Northwest Italian restaurants as well as her travels in Spain and around the Mediterranean. You can nibble on tapas or dig into paella. *256 Katlian St., Sitka; 907-966-3663.*

Westmark Sitka. Both the Kadataan Lounge and the Raven Dining Room in this modern, upscale hotel focus on seafood. Try the blackened or cedar-planked salmon. This used to be called the Shee Atika, so if you're asking for directions you may need to use its old name. *330 Seward St., Sitka; 907-747-6241 or 800-544-0970; www.westmarkhotels.com.*

■ GETTING AROUND

Towns along the Inside Passage are in some ways isolated, as most lack highway and rail infrastructure. In fact, there is only one mile of road for every 44 square miles of land, and only 32 percent of that road is paved.

However, the Alaska Marine Highway, the state's ferry system, links the communities of the Inside Passage via its regular 1,048-mile circuit. The "Big Blue Canoes" sail from Bellingham, Washington, to Skagway. The breathtaking scenery along this circuit earned it a National Scenic Byway designation in 2002. Reservations should be confirmed six months in advance (www.state.ak.us/amhshome.html; 800-642-0066). Some visitors drive to Skagway or Haines and get aboard the ferry there. Ferries have excellent dining rooms, with hot beverages generally available at all times. Locals tend to take no-frills trips, camping on deck, but there are also cabins available. AMH now has a couple of faster ferries. Be sure to inquire about whether you're getting the "milk run" or the speedier craft.

The more touristed Inside Passage towns have tours tracing a specified route, and for the price of a ticket you can get off and re-board at any of their regular stops in your own good time. On the other hand, if you draw up a list of preferred destinations in advance, a taxi driver can customize your tour. (Contact the local chamber of commerce or visitors bureau for taxi recommendations.) Bicycle rentals are generally available, but bike paths may be skimpy, under construction, or repurposed, unpaved logging roads.

Most cruise-ship lines and tour operators own their own sightseeing buses, which will be omnipresent at cruise-ship docks. Gray Line of Alaska (800-544-2206; www.graylineofalaska.com) offers coach tours and connections to such activities as whale-watching and Mendenhall River float trips out of Juneau and a Totem Bight tour out of Ketchikan. If you have not made up your mind about excursions before arriving, spontaneous decisions may be made on the spot. In fact, locals are not allowed on some excursions, in order to keep all seats for tourists.

Then there are the bush flights or air taxis. It could be as simple as a 20-minute flight with just you, a companion, the pilot, and three seats of groceries. But caveat emptor: flight services tend to hire summer-season pilots who are unused to Alaskan flight conditions. Before buying a ticket, it pays to ask the pilot about how long he or she's been in flying in the area, so you can pick someone with local experience.

■ Gold Panning

Prospectors have investigated nearly every water course in Alaska for gold. And many waterways will yield that precious metal—albeit in infinitesimal flakes. Gold panning and other recreational mining activities are permitted on most public lands and in rivers classified "wild," but be sure to contact parkland managers and don't trespass on property posted "private." If panning is a must-try on your list, check with the local visitors center for creeks where this activity is allowed.

At its most basic, panning is sloshing water, dirt, and gravel around in large pie plates. Gold is very heavy, so as you slosh away the lighter dirt and gravel the shiny precious metal will be left behind in your pan. First scoop the gravel you want to prospect into your pan. Then shake the pan in a left-to-right motion under water. Lighter materials will be washed away.

Alaska Travel Adventures (800-791-2673 outside Alaska; 800-478-0052 inside Alaska; www.alaskaadventures.com) offers gold panning in Juneau. During Juneau's A-J Mine/Gastineau Mill tour (907-463-3900) you will have a chance to pan for gold (guaranteed in every pan). In Juneau, Goldbelt Tours also offers gold panning with guaranteed gold in every pan (907-586-8687; www.goldbelttours.com). Hobbyist panners with their own sluice boxes pan for free in Juneau's Gold Creek at Cope Park.

To study up on panning methods in advance, check the Web site of The New 49'ers Club, www.goldgold.com.

■ LODGING AND CAMPING

Lodging of all sorts is available along the Inside Passage—whether you're looking for a barebones cabin, a dormitory-type hostel, or all the bells and whistles like cable modem access and an in-room whirlpool tub.

In many towns you can find hotels in historic buildings. (In Haines you can even stay in Fort William H. Seward, at Hotel Halsingland.) There's a good sprinkling of fishing lodges too, in places like Prince of Wales Island and Baranof Island. There aren't too many chains around; Westmark Hotels focuses on Alaska and the Yukon. Hotel rates drop significantly during off-season, sometimes 25 percent or more.

For bed-and-breakfasts, vacation homes, cabins, and lodges throughout the Southeast, get in touch with Alaska Travelers Accommodations (800-928-3308; www.AlaskaTravelers.com), a reservations service. Or try the Bed & Breakfast Association of Alaska (www.inns-alaska.com). If you want a kitchenette, you may need to make reservations months in advance. (Wilderness cabins are equipped with kitchens, but you will probably need to bring your own camping stove and heating fuel.) There are also a couple of locally focused services, such as the Web site www.accommodations-alaska.com, which lists Inside Passage B&Bs, country inns, and small lodges by city. Ketchikan Reservation Service (800-987-5337; www.ketchikan-lodging.com) handles reservations in the Ketchikan area.

The U.S. Forest Service rents rustic cabins sleeping 6 to 16 in many areas, for $35 a night. Call the National Recreation Reservation Service at 877-444-6777. Some cabins are accessed via hiking trails; others require kayak, boat, or pontoon-equipped bush plane access. State parks also offers cabins at $25 a night; call 907-465-4563 or log on to www.dnr.state.ak.us/parks/index.htm.

Most of the larger Inside Passage towns have RV parks and campgrounds, including Juneau, Wrangell, Petersburg, Sitka, and Skagway. There are campsites at state parks and national parks in the Haines area. For low-tech travelers exploring with knapsack in the European style, Ketchikan and Sitka both have hostels affiliated with Hostelling International (202-783-6161; ww.hiusa.org); other towns, including Juneau, Petersburg, and Skagway, have privately owned hostels.

Cruise ships ease into Juneau's Gastineau Channel.

■ SHOPPING

Shop wisely. There's a lot of made-in-China schlock out there. If you wish to purchase Native-made art or crafts, make sure they come with a certification tag or ask for a guarantee penned on your sales slip. The Silver Hand tag assures authenticity, with the words "Native Handicraft from Alaska." The name of the artist may be penned in. The Made in Alaska emblem guarantees the piece was made in the state—but not necessarily by a Native (www.dced.state.ak.us/dca/mia/home.htm).

For details, read the brochure *Alaskan Native Art* put out by the Alaska Attorney General's Office and the Alaska State Council on the Arts (888-278-7424; www. educ.state.ak.us/aksca/). For more about traditional and contemporary Native art, access www.alaskanativeartists.com, a site dedicated to promoting Native artists.

Don't fret over lugging a 20-foot totem or 150-pound bronze. Most galleries ship, even in smaller places like the village of Metlakatla.

One tasty souvenir you can find all over the Inside Passage is syrup from Birch Boy Products (907-767-5660; www.birchboy.com). This company produces more than 20 natural syrups you can use on waffles and ice cream. The most unusual may be birch, but they also bottle spruce tip, rhubarb, highbush cranberry, and Russian-American cherry (based on sour cherries planted in Sitka by Russian settlers).

■ ANN'S FAVORITE SHOPS

Ketchikan.
Hit the Soho Coho Gallery (5 Creek Street; 907-225-5954; www.trollart.com) to see Ray Troll's zany T-shirts, wonderful books, limited edition serigraphs, and "fish juju." Ray's mischievous slogan is "better living through difficult art." His refrigerator magnets turn up in supermarkets all over Southeast Alaska. Another artist who exhibits here is Evon Zerbetz; check out her greeting cards and children's books, as well as originals.

Ketchikan offers competing spots for one-stop shopping: Spruce Mill Mall and Salmon Landing Market. Both are in-your-face places next to the cruise-ship dock. Window-shop here for fabric for quilters, silver jewelry, beads, and local art such as linocuts and block prints. To immerse yourself in art, hightail it to Alaska Eagle Art Gallery (5 Creek Street; 907-225-8365) for exquisite work by Quinault/Isleta-Pueblo artist Marvin Oliver. Go to Crazy Wolf Studio (697 Mission Street; 907-225-9653) for carvings by Tsimshian Ken Decker. For carvings by Tlingit master Norman G. Jackson, head for Ketchikan's Carver on the Creek (Creek and

Stedman streets; 907-225-3018). Jackson is a recognized master of both woodcarving and metal engraving.

Petersburg.
If you don't want to go home without a Norwegian or Icelandic sweater, drop by Lee's Clothing (207 Nordic Drive; 907-772-4229).

Juneau.
Head for Raven's Journey (439 South Franklin Street; 907-463-4686) or Hummingbird Hollow (Juneau Airport; 907-789-4672) for outstanding collectibles. Both offer tasteful traditional works in walrus ivory, whalebone, copper, and wood, as well as Native dolls and modern art glass.

Sitka.
Because of the town's Russian heritage, amber and *pysanki* (intricately decorated Russian Easter eggs) are common items. Seek out the Sitka Rose Gallery (Lincoln Street; 888-236-1536), next door to the Russian Bishop's House, and you'll not only get the chance to enter a century-old residence but also to browse among sculpture, paintings, beadwork, and jewelry. The Sheldon Jackson Museum shop is another worthwhile browsing destination.

■ SURVIVAL

Alaska's terrain can be unforgiving. **Don't take the risks lightly.** Every year people drown, become disoriented and lost, suffer from hypothermia, or fall to their deaths. Check with the Forest Service when planning a hiking, camping, canoeing, or kayaking outing. Obtain trail maps, permits, and weather reports before heading out. Ask about bear density—and recent bear sightings. Take sufficient clothing, food, and water. If your knees and ankles wobble a bit, use trekking poles. Carry a VHF hand-held radio on extended kayak trips. Leave a detailed float or flight plan behind so someone will alert search and rescue (SAR) authorities if you're late returning. If the weather looks at all threatening, don't push ahead. And don't rely on cell phones, as they may not work in remote areas.

Do your best to **prevent hypothermia.** Hypothermia is a decrease in the body's core temperature to a level at which normal physical and mental functions are impaired. Severe hypothermia can be fatal. Avoid it by wearing layers of clothing (including a windbreaker), changing wet clothing for dry, keeping hydrated, and avoiding fatigue. Warning symptoms include shivering, goose bumps, and accelerated heartbeat, followed by stumbling and slurred speech. If you notice any of these symptoms in yourself or a fellow traveler, stop to rest, layer on clothing, and drink water or something hot. Don't drink anything alcoholic, as this speeds heat loss.

Giardia, an intestinal parasite that can cause cramps and diarrhea, is common in Alaskan streams and rivers. Boil, filter, or chemically treat all water you use.

When kayaking, fishing, canoeing, or traveling in a small boat, wear a life jacket. Keep in mind that ocean swells, opposing currents, rapids, and boat wakes can sink small craft. Alaskan waters are extremely cold; death is almost certain within 15 minutes of immersion. Consult a tide book before setting out. (Tide tables for Juneau, Ketchikan, and Sitka are printed in PDC's Southeast Alaska phone book.)

Watch your footing. Many trails are narrow, with steep drop-offs, unstable footing, fractured rock, mossy logs, roots, or slippery slate. It's very easy to sprain an ankle and be stranded. Consider carrying a police whistle to signal for help.

If you have been dropped off at a remote site by a bush plane, keep in mind that weather and visibility can delay scheduled pickups.

■ TIME

Southeast Alaska is on Alaska Time, one hour earlier than Pacific Time.

■ USEFUL CONTACTS

All emergencies: 911.
Area code for the entire state of Alaska: 907.
Fish and Game licensing: 907-465-2376.
Time and temperature: 907-586-3185 (for Juneau) or www.inalaska.com/alaska/ weather (entire state).
U.S. Coast Guard: 800-478-5555 for Maritime Search and Rescue; 800-478-6381 for boating registration.
U.S. Customs: 907-586-7211; www.customs.gov.
Weather in Alaska: 800-472-0391 (National Weather Service).

■ CRUISE LINES

American Safari Cruises: 888-862-8881; www.amsafari.com.
American West Steamboat Company: 800-434-1232; www.columbiarivercruise.com.
Carnival Cruise Lines: 800-227-6482; www.carnival.com.

Celebrity Cruises: 800-437-3111; www.celebrity.com.
Clipper Cruise Line: 800-325-0010; www.clippercruise.com.
Cruise West: 800-888-9378; www.cruisewest.com.
Crystal Cruises: 800-820-6663; www.crystalcruises.com.
Glacier Bay Cruise Line: 800-451-5952; www.glacierbaytours.com.
Holland America Westours: 877-724-5425; www.hollandamerica.com.
Linblad Expeditions: 800-397-3348; www.expeditions.com.
Norwegian Cruise Lines: 800-327-7030; www.ncl.com.
Princess Cruises: 800-774-6237; www.princess.com.
Radisson Seven Seas Cruises: 877-505-5370; www.rssc.com.
Royal Caribbean Cruise Line: 800-327-6700; www.royalcaribbean.com.

■ TRANSPORTATION

Alaska Airlines: 800-252-7522; www.alaskaair.com.
Alaska Fjordlines: 800-320-0146; www.alaskafjordlines.com; passenger-only ferry service between Haines, Juneau, and Skagway from late May through August.
Alaska Marine Highway Reservations: 800-642-0066; TDD, 800-764-3779; www.alaska.gov/ferry.
Alaska Rent-A-Car: 800-662-0007; www.akcarrental.com.
Budget Rent A Car: 800-527-0700 for worldwide reservations; www.budget.com.
Chilkat Cruises: 907-766-2100; www.chilkatcruises.com; ferry service between Haines and Skagway from May through September.
ERA Aviation, Inc.: 907-586-2030.
Fjord Flying Service, Gustavus: 907-697-2377.
Harris Aircraft Services Inc., Sitka: 907-966-3050.
Ketchikan Air: 907-225-6608.
Kupreanof Flying Service: 907-772-3396.
L.A.B. Flying Service Inc.: 907-766-2222; http://labflying.com/.
Pacific Wing Air Charters, Petersburg: 907-772-4258.
Promech Air, Ketchikan: 907-225-3845.
Sunrise Aviation, Wrangell: 907-874-2319.
Taquan Air Alaska: 800-770-8800; http://taquanair.com.
Transportation Security Administration: www.TSATravelTips.us; tips on how to manage your luggage (e.g., what not to pack) when flying.
Ward Air Inc., Juneau: 907-789-9150.
Wings of Alaska Airlines: 907-789-0790; www.wingsofalaska.com.
Yakutat Coastal Airlines: 907-784-3831.

■ **VISITOR INFORMATION**

Alaska Department of Fish & Game, Division of Wildlife Conservation:
www.wildlifenews.alaska.gov; monthly online newsletter about everything from
Dolly Varden fish to coyotes.

Alaska Marine Highway: 800-642-0066; www.FerryAlaska.com.

Alaska Public Lands Information Center, Ketchikan: 907-228-6214; www.nps.
gov/aplic/.

Alaska Relay (telecommunications relay service for deaf, hard of hearing and
speech disabled): TTY 800-770-8973.

Alaska Scenic Byways Program: 907-465-8769; www.alaska.gov/scenic.

Alaska Travel Industry Information: www.travelalaska.com.

Challenge Alaska: 907-344-7399; www.challengealaska.org; information about
access for people with disabilities.

Glacier Bay National Park Service: 907-697-2230; www.nps.gov/glac/.

Gustavus Visitors Association (gateway to Glacier National Park): 907-697-2285;
www.gustavus.com.

Haines Convention & Visitors Bureau: 800-458-3579; www.haines.ak.us/.

Juneau Convention & Visitors Bureau: 888-581-2201; www.traveljuneau.com.

JuneauAlaska.com: www.juneaualaska.com; on-line visitor guide supported by the
Juneau Empire newspaper.

Ketchikan Ranger District/Misty Fiords National Monument: 907-225-2148;
www.fs.fed.us/r10/tongass/districts/ketchikan/ktnmisty.

Ketchikan Visitors Bureau: 907-225-6166; www.visit-ketchikan.com.

Klondike Gold Rush National Historical Park Visitor Center, Skagway: 907-983-
2921; www.nps.gov/klgo/.

Petersburg Visitor Information Center: 907-772-4636 or 866-484-4700;
www.petersburg.org.

Sitka Convention & Visitors Bureau: 907-747-5940; www.sitka.org.

Skagway Convention & Visitors Bureau: 907-983-2854; www.skagway.com.

Southeast Alaska Tourism Council: 907-586-5777; www.alaskainfo.org.

Tongass National Forest: 907-225-3101; www.fs.fed.us/r10/tongass/.

Wrangell Visitor Information: 907-874-3901 or 800-367-9745; www.wrangell.com
or www.wrangellchamber.org.

RECOMMENDED READING

Cape Fox Corporation, *A Time Remembered: Cape Fox Village 1899,* 1981. Photos by Edward Curtis from the Harriman Expedition are paired with brief text to rescue traditions and heritage from obscurity.

Clifford, Howard, *The Skagway Story,* 2003. Colorful characters and amusing anecdotes abound in this well-researched portrait of a city and its early history. It covers everything from trailblazing to hockey.

Drucker, Philip, *Cultures of the North Pacific Coast,* 1965. A comprehensive anthropological and sociological review of the culture of the Northwest Coast and its significance, including topics such as warfare and shamanism.

Emmons, George, and Frederica de Laguna, *The Tlingit Indians,* 1991. An ethnography with historical depth presented in chronological order. Learn about everything from houses to halibut fishing, from tools to potlatches.

Garfield, Viola, and Paul Wingert, *The Tsimshian Indians and Their Arts,* 1973. A summary of Tsimshian society, religion, mythology, dance, arts, and crafts.

Howard, Jim, *Guide to Sea Kayaking in Southeast Alaska: The Best Day Trips and Tours from Misty Fjords to Glacier Bay,* 1999. A well-organized, nitty-gritty guide for planning both brief and extended excursions, with mile-by-mile descriptions and sidetrip options.

O'Clair, Rita, Robert H. Armstrong, and Richard Carstensen, *The Nature of Southeast Alaska,* 1997. The authors, all Juneau residents expert in their respective fields, serve forth facts about plants and animals illustrated with detailed pen-and-ink drawings.

Raban, Jonathan, *Passage to Juneau,* 2000. History meets personal travel narrative as the author recounts a boat trip through the Passage.

Smith, Dave, *Backcountry Bear Basics,* 1997. A concise guide to safe behavior, food storage, etc., when bushwacking, camping, and kayaking in wilderness areas.

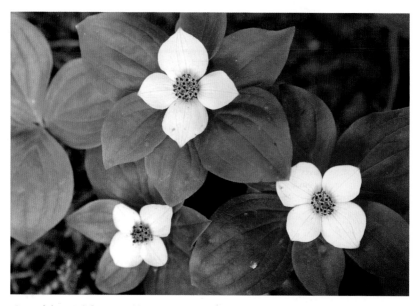

Ground dogwood flowers in bloom.

Stewart, Hilary, *Stone, Bone, Antler & Shell: Artifacts of the Northwest Coast,* 1996. Heavily illustrated and easy-to-read text reveals much about traditional ways of life, including trading, foods, clothing, technologies, and art.

Wilson, Graham, *The Klondike Gold Rush: Photographs from 1896–1899,* 1997. More than a hundred archival images document the "last great adventure" and illustrate the life of the average stampeder.

Wilson, Graham, *The Last Great Gold Rush: A Klondike Reader,* 2002. The "strange things done under the midnight sun" are described by participants, including Robert Service, Jack London, Emma Kelly, Tappan Adney, Frederick Schwatka, Rex Beach, and Arthur Walden.

I N D E X

Many sites and attractions listed below are followed by an abbreviation indicating the town/island/preserve in which each is found: (GBNP)=Glacier Bay National Park and Preserve; (H)=Haines; (J)=Juneau; (K)=Ketchikan; (MFNM)=Misty Fiords National Monument; (POW)=Prince of Wales Island; (Sit)=Sitka; (Sk)=Skagway; (TNF)=Tongass National Forest; (W)=Wrangell.

COMPASS AMERICAN GUIDES

Alaska

Alaska's Inside Passage

American Southwest

Arizona

Boston

California Wine Country

Cape Cod

Chicago

Coastal California

Colorado

Connecticut & Rhode Island

Florida

Georgia

Gulf South

Hawaii

Idaho

Kentucky

Las Vegas

Maine

Manhattan

Massachusetts

Michigan

Minnesota

Montana

Montréal

Nevada

New Hampshire

New Mexico

New Orleans

North Carolina

Ohio

Oregon

Oregon Wine Country

Pacific Northwest

Pennsylvania

San Francisco

Santa Fe

South Carolina

South Dakota

Tennessee

Texas

Utah

Vermont

Virginia

Washington Wine Country

Wisconsin

Wyoming

COMPASS AMERICAN GUIDES

Critics, booksellers, and travelers all agree: you're lost without a Compass.

"This splendid series provides exactly the sort of historical and cultural detail about North American destinations that curious-minded travelers need."
—*Washington Post*

"This is a series that constantly stuns us . . . no guide with photos this good should have writing this good. But it does." —*New York Daily News*

"Of the many guidebooks on the market, few are as visually stimulating, as thoroughly researched, or as lively written as the Compass American Guide series."
—*Chicago Tribune*

"Good to read ahead of time, then take along so you don't miss anything."
—*San Diego Magazine*

"Magnificent photography. First rate."—*Money*

"Written by longtime residents of each destination . . . these handsome and literate guides are strong on history and culture, and illustrated with gorgeous photos."
—*San Francisco Chronicle*

"The color photographs sparkle, the archival illustrations illuminate windows to the past, and the writing is usually of the utmost caliber." —*Michigan Tribune*

"Class acts, worth reading and shelving for keeps even if you're not a traveler. "
—*New Orleans Times-Picayune*

"Beautiful photographs and literate writing are the hallmarks of the Compass guides." —*Nashville Tennessean*

"History, geography, and wanderlust converge in these well-conceived books."
—*Raleigh News & Observer*

"Oh, my goodness! What a gorgeous series this is."—*Booklist*

ACKNOWLEDGMENTS

■ FROM THE AUTHOR AND PHOTOGRAPHER

Ann Chandonnet wishes to thank Ellen Carrlee, Curator of Collections and Exhibits at the Juneau-Douglas City Museum, and Steve Henrikson, Curator of the Alaska State Museum, for their generous and enthusiastic help. She is also grateful to the staffs of other museums and visitors' centers throughout southeast Alaska for their invaluable aid in compiling and sorting through material for this book. Without the expertise of others, it would be impossible to encapsulate the varied history and scenic glories of the Inside Passage. Further thanks to Don Pitcher for laboring in the mines (literally) to capture unique angles of the landscape.

Don Pitcher would like to thank the following people for their assistance in photographing this book: David Allen and Joanne Witta from Goldbelt, Inc.; Michael Brandt from White Pass & Yukon Route Railway; Jim Collins from Allen Marine Tours; Steve Halloran from Glacier Bay Lodge & Tours; Len Lawrence from Inter-Island Ferry Authority; and Kathryn "Ryn" Schneider from Alaska Island Hostel.

■ FROM THE PUBLISHER

Compass American Guides would like to thank the following individuals or institutions for the use of their illustrations or photographs:

All photographs in this book are by Don Pitcher unless noted below.

Introduction:
Page 14, National Archives and Records Administration

The Land and the People:
Page 18, Museum of History and Industry, Seattle
Page 22, Alaska State Library
Page 25, Barry J. McWayne/University of Alaska Museum of the North (UA69-061-0001)
Page 26, Alaska State Museum (2000-39-1)
Page 27, Alaska State Museum (96-61-1)
Page 28, Alaska State Library

Ketchikan:
Page 33 (bottom), Eric Luse/Alaska Division of Tourism
Page 34, Alaska State Library, Skinner Foundation Collection
Page 40, Alaska State Library, Skinner Foundation Collection

Petersburg:
Page 70, Michael S. Nolan/age fotostock

Juneau:
Page 82, Alaska State Library, Skinner Foundation Collection

Skagway:
Page 112, University of Washington Libraries, Special Collections (Hegg 156)
Page 116 (top), University of Alaska Fairbanks, Archives, James Bernard Moore (76-35-70)
Page 116 (bottom), University of Washington Libraries, Special Collections (Hegg 541)

Haines:
Page 127 (bottom), Alaska State Library
Page 128, Alaska State Library
Page 134, University of Washington Libraries, Special Collections (NA 2894)
Page 140 (bottom left), Alaska State Library, Skinner Foundation Collection

Glacier Bay National Park and Preserve:
Page 145 (top), Alaska State Library, Alaska State Library, Winter and Pond Collection

Sitka:
Page 153, Library of Congress Prints and Photographs Division
Page 156, Alaska State Library, Merrill Collection
Page 159 (bottom), Alaska State Library, Winter and Pond Collection

■ ABOUT THE AUTHOR

Ann Chandonnet has written extensively on lifestyles, food history, and the arts for newspapers and magazines on the West Coast. She has lived in Alaska for more than 30 years—since 1999 in the capital, Juneau. With her husband Fernand, Ann has explored the state on foot and snowshoes as well as by plane, helicopter, ferry, canoe, kayak, and fishing boat. She is the author of more than a dozen books, including *The Alaska Heritage Seafood Cookbook, Alaska's Arts, Crafts & Collectibles*, and *Gold Rush Grub*. An inveterate book reviewer, she also spends time substitute teaching, gardening, and quilting.

■ ABOUT THE PHOTOGRAPHER

After receiving a master's degree in fire ecology from the University of California at Berkeley, **Don Pitcher** spent 15 summers in the wilds of Alaska and Wyoming. His assignments encompassed everything from mapping grizzly habitat to operating salmon weirs—anything to avoid an office job. He now works as a photographer and travel writer, plotting his travels from Homer, Alaska, where he lives with his wife Karen Shemet and their children Aziza and Rio. Pitcher also photographed the Compass guide to Wyoming, and is the author of comprehensive travel guides for Alaska, Wyoming, Washington, Yellowstone, and the San Juan Islands. His images have appeared in a multitude of other publications and advertisements, and his prints are available in Alaskan galleries. Find details on his latest projects at www.donpitcher.com.